AF564658

BRIDGING BORDERS

India-Nepal Relations in a Changing Geopolitical Landscape

BRIDGING BORDERS

India-Nepal Relations in a Changing Geopolitical Landscape

Lieutenant General Shokin Chauhan
PVSM, AVSM, YSM, SM, VSM, PhD

Foreword by

General Anil Chauhan
PVSM, UYSM, AVSM, SM, VSM
Chief of Defence Staff

PENTAGON PRESS LLP

First published in 2024 by
PENTAGON PRESS LLP
206, Peacock Lane, Shahpur Jat
New Delhi-110049, India
Contact: 011-64706243

Typeset in Adobe Garamond, 11.5 Point
Printed by Aegean Offset Printers, Greater Noida, U.P.

ISBN 978-81-968722-7-4 (HB)

www.pentagonpress.in

CONTENTS

FOREWORD

1. It is with great pleasure and honor that I introduce this seminal work by my esteemed friend, General Shokin Chauhan, on the intricate dynamics of the Indo-Nepal strategic relationship. The General Officer's comprehensive exploration of the historical, geographical and contemporary dimensions of this crucial bilateral relationship is a testament to his deep understanding, unwavering dedication and invaluable experience. His distinguished career in the military, coupled with his tenure as the military attaché in the Indian Embassy in Kathmandu, Nepal, uniquely positions him to offer insightful original authentic suggestions.

2. The book, takes the reader on a journey through time, unraveling the historical ties that have bound India and Nepal together for centuries. From ancient trade routes to cultural exchanges, the narrative paints a vivid picture of the deep-rooted connections that have shaped the Indo-Nepal relationship. By delving into the historical context, it lays the groundwork for understanding the complexities and nuances of the present-day strategic landscape.

3. The author's analysis of the strategic geography of the region also provides invaluable insights. Detailed maps, case studies and strategic assessments elucidate the significance of Nepal's unique position as a buffer state between two regional powers and its implications for regional stability and security.

4. Drawing on his first hand experience and extensive research, the General Officer offers a candid assessment of the challenges that have strained the bilateral relationship in recent years. From border disputes to political tensions, he confronts the issues head-on, challenging readers to confront the complexities and nuances of interstate relations in South Asia.

.......2/-

5. The author's insights into the India-Nepal military relationship are particularly noteworthy. As a seasoned military officer with years of experience in the field, his analysis of defence cooperation, joint exercises and security challenges provides a rare glimpse into the inner workings of military diplomacy. By highlighting the strategic imperatives and mutual interests that underpin the India-Nepal military relationship, he offers a compelling argument for deeper engagement and cooperation between the two countries' armed forces.

6. Throughout the pages of this book, General Chauhan's passion for promoting peace, stability and cooperation in the Indo-Nepal relationship shines through. His dedication to fostering understanding and dialogue is evident in every word, making this book not only a scholarly endeavour but also a call to action for policymakers, scholars and citizens alike.

7. In conclusion, the book is a tour de force that offers a comprehensive, nuanced and insightful analysis of the Indo-Nepal strategic relationship. It is my sincere hope that this book sparks meaningful conversations, fosters greater understanding and lays the groundwork for a more peaceful and prosperous future for India and Nepal, and indeed, for the entire South Asian region.

Jai Hind!

(Anil Chauhan)
General
Chief of Defence Staff

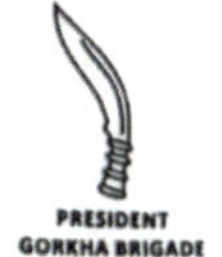

PRESIDENT
GORKHA BRIGADE

XI GORKHA RIFLES
वज्राई विजयस्तत

FIRST BN

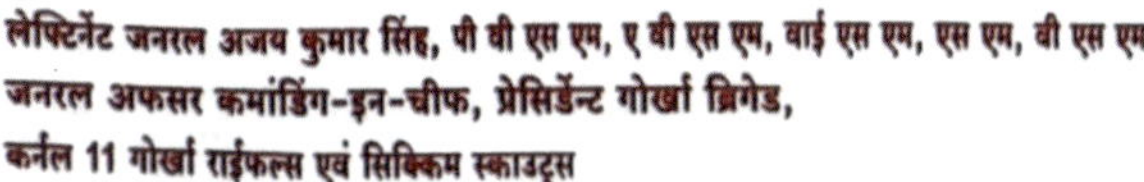
लेफ्टिनेंट जनरल अजय कुमार सिंह, पी वी एस एम, ए वी एस एम, वाई एस एम, एस एम, वी एस एम
जनरल अफसर कमांडिंग-इन-चीफ, प्रेसिडेंट गोर्खा ब्रिगेड,
कर्नल 11 गोर्खा राईफल्स एवं सिक्किम स्काउट्स

Lt Gen Ajai Kumar Singh, PVSM, AVSM, YSM, SM, VSM
General Officer Commanding-in-Chief, President Gorkha Brigade,
Colonel 11 GR & Sikkim Scouts

मुख्यालय
दक्षिणी कमान
पिन - 908541
द्वारा 56 ए पी ओ

Headquarters
Southern Command
PIN - 908541
c/o 56 APO

MESSAGE FROM PRESIDENT GORKHA BRIGADE

In the intricate tapestry of India-Nepal relations, one thread that stands out prominently is the unwavering contribution of the Gorkhas of Nepal. As we celebrate the rich history and deep-rooted ties between our two nations, it is paramount to acknowledge the invaluable role played by the Gorkha community in fostering and strengthening this bond. The Gorkhas, renowned for their valor, loyalty, and resilience, have left an indelible mark on the history of both India and Nepal. Their contributions span various domains, from the battlefield to the socio-cultural fabric, enriching the uniqueness of our shared heritage.

As India embarks on her journey of *Amrit Kaal* aspiring to become a developed nation by 2047, its relations with its neighbours will be of paramount importance for regional stability, economic prosperity and security. Fostering strong and cooperative relationships with neighbouring countries and in particular Nepal is crucial for India's development and overall peace and prosperity of the region. Nurturing positive and constructive relationships with neighbours is imperative and will remain a cornerstone of India's foreign policy in future.

The ties between India and Nepal, traditionally built on trust, mutual support, and people-to-people interactions, encompass historical, economic, religious, and socio-cultural connections. The constant movement of populations across open borders has historically fortified this relationship. At the heart of the Gorkha legacy lies their exemplary service in the Indian Army. Nepal Domiciled Gorkhas have been the epitome of valour and bravery and have deep historical connect with India for over two centuries. Gorkha regiments have stood shoulder to shoulder with and as part of Indian forces, safeguarding our borders and upholding the principles of peace and security. They have participated in all campaigns of war as an integral part of Indian Army and Gorkha Rifles are the most decorated units where in their exceptional performance across all aspects of military operations has consistently set a benchmark for excellence. Their courage and dedication have earned them admiration and respect across the nation, symbolizing the deep-rooted friendship between our peoples.

Nepal Domicile Gorkha Soldiers and veterans form a crucial pillar of Indo-Nepal relations and serve as goodwill ambassadors, bridging the gap between India and Nepal through their vibrant connect with the Indian Army. They have shown exemplary zeal, enthusiasm, and honesty in implementing various welfare schemes sponsored by Government of India which has not only enhanced their status in society but also created more than one lakh ambassadors for Brand India and the values that it stands for. Their presence in both nations serves as a living testament to the enduring ties that bind us together, transcending borders and fostering mutual understanding and harmony.

Distinguished military service and being former Military Attache in Nepal, Gen Shokin Chauhan has been endowed with immeasurable hands on experience, profound comprehension and nuanced perspective wherein he has intricately weaved the insightful analysis of our complex bilateral relationship. *Bridging Borders India - Nepal Relations in a changing Geopolitical Landscape* delves into the intricate and historically rich relationship between India and Nepal, shedding light on bilateral relations under the backdrop of Chinese influence, its multifaceted dimensions and significance in changing geopolitical landscape. The book offers comprehensive analysis of cultural, economic, political, military security and strategic ties between the two nations. It also examines Sino-Nepalese relations and its impact on India's relations and meticulously suggests recommendations that underscore the importance of fostering mutual understanding, cooperation, and trust between India and Nepal.

As we reflect on the journey of India-Nepal relations in the evolving geopolitical landscape, we must acknowledge the pivotal role played by the Gorkhas. Their sacrifices, contributions, and enduring legacy serve as a beacon of hope and inspiration, reminding us of the unbreakable bonds of friendship and cooperation that exist between our nations.

Let us reaffirm our commitment to nurturing and strengthening the bonds of friendship between India and Nepal, honoring the invaluable contributions of the Gorkha community. Together, we can build a future marked by peace, prosperity, and mutual respect, embodying the spirit of unity in diversity that defines our relationship.

'Jai Hind'

(Ajai Kumar Singh)
Lt Gen
GOC-in-C

Station : Pune

Date 08 Mar 2024

Preface

In the era of global interconnectivity, the intricate dance of geopolitical forces profoundly influences the destinies of nations. This book, *Bridging Borders*, is a compelling exploration into the complex interplay between India and Nepal in the 21st century, where diplomatic intricacies intersect with the challenges posed by an increasingly assertive China. This work serves as a timely and insightful analysis, unravelling the multifaceted dimensions of India's strategic relations with Nepal set against the backdrop of the subtle yet impactful ingress of Chinese influence into Nepal's political and economic landscape.

As the pages unfold, readers will embark on a journey through the historical tapestry that binds India and Nepal together, delving into deep-rooted cultural affinities, historical ties, geographical proximity, and a unique military relationship shaped by the presence of Nepali-origin soldiers in the Indian armed forces. These elements form the foundation of the unique and ancient relationship between two neighbouring countries. This book meticulously scrutinizes China's subtle manoeuvres, and provides a nuanced perspective on its expanding footprint in Nepal and the potential implications for upsetting the delicate balance in South Asian geopolitics, potentially leading to conflict.

The narrative is meticulously woven with research, offering a comprehensive understanding of the diplomatic, military, economic, and strategic dimensions at play. This book engages with the evolving nature of India-Nepal relations, and explores the challenges and opportunities arising as the region navigates the complexities of the 21st century. As the author deeply committed to fostering informed discourse, I have endeavoured to produce a work that aims to bridge the gap in understanding, providing readers, scholars, and policymakers with a valuable resource to comprehend the intricate dance of interests and influences shaping the geopolitical landscape of South Asia.

Lieutenant General Shokin Chauhan

ACKNOWLEDGEMENTS

I would like to acknowledge the extraordinary debt I owe to my soldiers from Nepal who served alongside me. Their sacrifice, dedication, camaraderie, and shared experiences have enriched my understanding of the intricate dynamics that define the relationship between our nations. Their insights and perspectives have been invaluable in shaping the narrative of this book.

To all those who have contributed, be it through shared experiences, intellectual discussions, or moral support, my sincere thanks. Writing this book has been a collaborative effort, and your influence resonates through its pages. As we navigate the intricate tapestry of international relations, your contributions stand as a testament to the strength of collaborative endeavours and the importance of shared experiences in shaping our understanding of strategic alliances.

To my family – for a lifetime of unwavering support, thank you to my wife, Daphne, who has stood by me through all my travails and been my sounding board. To my son, Nihal, and daughter-in-law, Arami, who fill my heart with joy, thank you for always being there for me. Most of all, to my grandchildren, Ari and Kai, whose laughter is my favourite sound and makes everything wonderful!

Lieutenant General Shokin Chauhan

List of Maps

List of Abbreviations

ADB	Asian Development Bank
AIR	All India Radio
AMA (R)	Assistant Military Attaché (Record)
APECF	Asia Pacific Exchange and Cooperation Foundation
APT	ASEAN-Plus Three
ASA	Air Services Agreement
ASI	Archaeological Survey of India
BBIN	Bangladesh, Bhutan, India, Nepal Initiative
BDCCs	Border District Coordination Committees
BIMSTEC	Bay of Bengal Initiative for Multi-Sectoral Technical and Economic Cooperation
BIPPA	Bilateral Investment Promotion and Protection Agreement
BRI	Belt and Road Initiative
BWG	Boundary Working Group
CA	Constituent Assembly
CI	Civilian Integration
COAS	Chief of the Army Staff
CPA	Comprehensive Peace Agreement
CPAO	Central Pension Accounting Officer
CPN (Maoist Centre)	Communist Party of Nepal (Maoist Centre)
CPN-UML	Communist Party of Nepal (Unified Marxist-Leninist)

CSC	China Study Centres
CVD	Countervailing Duty
DSBs	District Soldier Boards
DTAA	Double Taxation Avoidance Agreement
EAS	East Asia Summit
ECHS	Ex-Servicemen Contributory Health Scheme
EFP	Enhanced Family Pension
ESM	Ex-Servicemen
FDI	Foreign Direct Investment
GHQ India	General Headquarters India
GRTU	Gorkha Resettlement Training Unit
HADR	Humanitarian Aid and Disaster Relief
ICPs	Integrated Check Posts
IEWON	Indian Ex-Servicemen's Welfare Organisation in Nepal
IMF	International Monetary Fund
IMM	Indian Military Mission
IMTAG	Indian Military Training and Advisory Group
INA	Indian National Army
ISI	Inter-Services Intelligence
ITBP	Indo-Tibetan Border Police
JCWR	Joint Committee on Water Resources
JMCWR	Joint Ministerial Commission for Water Resources
JSC	Joint Steering Committee
JSTC	Joint Standing Technical Committee
JTLBC	Joint Technical Level Boundary Committee
JTT	Joint Technical Team
JWG	Joint Working Group
MEA	Ministry of External Affairs
MI	Military Integration

NA	Nepal Army
NAM	Non-aligned Movement
NATO	North Atlantic Treaty Organization
NC	Nepali Congress
NDG	Nepal Domiciled Gorkha
NEA	Nepal Electricity Authority
NEFA	North-East Frontier Agency
NOK	Next of Kin
NWF	North West Frontier
PCDA	Principal Controller of Defence Accounts
PDA	Pension Distributing Authority
PLA	People's Liberation Army
PPOs	Pension Paying Offices
PPP	Purchasing Power Parity
PRC	People's Republic of China
RBI	Reserve Bank of India
RNA	Royal Nepalese Army
ROIE	Record Office in the Indian Embassy
RPP	Rashtriya Prajatantra Party
RSA	Rail Services Agreement
SAARC	South Asian Association for Regional Cooperation
SAPTA	SAARC Preferential Trading Arrangement
SCIP	Standing Committee on Inundation Problem
SJVN	Satluj Jal Vidyut Nigam
SMEs	Small and Medium Enterprises
SPPCs	Seasonal Pension Paying Camps
TAR	Tibet Autonomous Region
UCPN-M	Unified Communist Party of Nepal (Maoist)
UHNWIs	Ultra-High-Net-Worth Individuals

UN	United Nations
UNMIN	United Nations Mission in Nepal
UT	Union Territories
WTC	World Trade Centers
WWI	First World War
WWII	Second World War
YCL	Young Communist League

INTRODUCTION
HISTORICAL PERSPECTIVE

A Connected Subcontinent

South Asia or Southern Asia comprising Afghanistan, Bangladesh, Bhutan, the Maldives, Nepal, India, Pakistan, and Sri Lanka is ethnically diverse, with more than 2,000 ethnic entities with populations ranging from hundreds of millions to small tribal groups.[1] The region is ethnically very diverse in terms of its linguistic, social, cultural, and religious affiliations. Though ethnically diverse, the region evolved a shared cultural ambience[2] while still retaining its distinctive cultural beliefs and practices, which in turn, has been shaped by centuries of pre-historic and historical developments in the Indian subcontinent. An understanding of these historical developments is important especially in the present context, given that the notion of South Asia itself is recent and the product of a turbulent past.

Over the centuries, the region has been invaded and settled by many ethnic groups, including various Dravidian, Indo-Aryan and Iranian groups. The amalgamation of Dravidian, Indo-Aryan and native societies has produced composite cultures with many common traditions and beliefs that converge or diverge throughout the course of time, at times giving rise to strong local traditions. Cultural assimilation in terms of language, religion, art, and socio-political ideologies has been important components of such expansions. For instance, most of South Asia uses various abugidas of Braahmi origin in their scripts while languages such as Urdu, Pashto, and Sindhi use derivatives of the Perso-Arabic script. Not all languages in South Asia follow this strict dichotomy, though. For example, Kashmiri is written in both the Perso-Arabic script and in the Devanagari script. The same can be said for Punjabi, which is written in both Shahmukhi and Gurmukhi. Dhivehi is written in a script called Tana that shows characteristics of both the Arabic alphabets and of an abugida.[3] Besides, among the other nations, both India and Nepal show a great diversity in language with more than twenty-six distinct languages spoken in Nepal that are related to the Indo-European, Tibeto-Burman, and Austro-Asiatic language families[4] and twenty-two officially recognised scheduled languages in India belonging to various language families.[5]

Similarly, adherents of every major religion in the world can be found in the subcontinent[6] with Hinduism, Islam, and Buddhism being the dominant religions in the region. Historically, the fusion of Indo-Aryan Vedic religion with native South Asian non Vedic Shramana traditions and other Dravidian and local tribal beliefs gave rise to the ancient religions of Hinduism, Jainism and Buddhism and much later to Sikhism, when the Sufi tradition of Islam also significantly influenced the nascent Sikhism and its holiest scripture. Islam was introduced to the region through the Iranian rulers and now constitutes one of the major religions in most of these countries. Besides these religions, the region also has significant Christian and other religious minorities.

Generally, South Asia is often presumed to be India-centric. This may be attributed to the fact that India is the largest and the most populous country in the region, besides being the largest democracy in the world. It is also one of the fastest growing economies of the world and is politically, technologically, and militarily better equipped than the other nations in the region.

As much as it is true that India is the dominant country of the region, it is not only a result of its geographical size or economic wealth but also an outcome of its significant historical heritage and developments in the past.

A Shared History

South Asia includes the present-day political entities of the Indian subcontinent and associated islands; therefore, its history includes the histories of India, Pakistan, Bangladesh, Nepal, Afghanistan, Bhutan, and the island nations of Sri Lanka and the Maldives. Although all these histories are often interlinked. Although all these historics are often interlinked, discussed will be the deep-rooted history between India and Nepal.

The history of a people is the story of their survival and growth on the land.[7] The stories of both India and Nepal in this respect have undergone tremendous changes since the earliest times. Nepal's recorded history began with the Kiratis, who arrived in the seventh or eighth century BCE from the east of Asia. It was during this period that Buddhism first came to the country; indeed, it is claimed that Buddha and his disciple Ananda visited the Kathmandu Valley and stayed for a while in Patan. By 200 CE, Buddhism had waned, and was replaced by Hinduism, brought by the Licchavis, who invaded from northern India and overthrew the last Kirati king. The Hindus also introduced the caste system and ushered the classical age of Nepalese art and architecture.

By 879 CE, the Licchavi era had petered out and was succeeded by the Thakuri dynasty. A grim period of instability and invasion often referred to as the Dark Ages followed, but the Kathmandu Valleys strategic location ensured the kingdoms survival and growth. Several centuries later, the Thakuri king, Arideva, founded the Malla dynasty, kick-starting another renaissance of Nepali/Hindu culture.

Nepal is frequently called the Gorkhali kingdom and takes its name from the legendary eighth-century Hindu warrior-saint Guru Gorakhnath.[8] They trace their ancestry to the Hindu Rajputs and Brahmins of north India who entered modern Nepal from the west following advances by the Muslims. In the village of Gorkha, about 50 miles west of Kathmandu, is a temple dedicated to Gorakhnath as well as another dedicated to Gorakhkali, a corresponding female deity.[9]

Prior to the 18th century, Nepal was a divided country but by 1769, under the leadership of King Dhiraj Prithvi Narayan Shahdev (1769-1775), the Gorkha dynasty had taken over the areas of modern Nepal[10] and this served as a driving force to unify Nepal. After his death, the Shah dynasty began to expand their kingdom into what is present day North India and Tibet. Between 1788 and 1791, Nepal invaded Tibet and robbed the

Tashilhunpo monastery of Shigatse. Tibet sought the help of the Chinese and Emperor Qianlong appointed Fu Kangan commander-in-chief of the Tibetan campaign. After a series of successful Chinese victories, Nepal signed a treaty on Chinese terms that required, among other obligations, that it send tribute to the Chinese emperor every five years.[11]

On the western side, the Kangra fort, now part of India's Himachal Pradesh, was captured by the Nepalese Army under the leadership of General Amar Singh Thapa who had succeeded in extending Nepal to the Sutlej River. By the early 19th century, Nepalese territory had stretched up to the banks of the Sutlej River in Punjab and Kumaon to the west and the Teesta River in the east.[12]

Nepal's Cultural Diversity-Ethenically Indian?

Nepal is an ethnically diverse and composite country whose physical composition and culture ranges from the Indian to the Tibetan. Except for the Terai region where the majority of the population is of Indian birth or parentage, the varied ethnic groups had developed into distinguishable forms over time.[13]

The Nepali population is divided into three major ethnic groups, namely, the Indo-Nepali, Tibeto-Nepali, and indigenous Nepali. The first two groups clearly indicate the direction of their migration in Nepal and most ethnic groups were found at particular altitudes.[14] The first group, constituting those of Indo-Nepali origin, dwelt in the more fertile lower hills, river valleys, and Terai fields. The second major group comprised of communities of Tibeto-Mongol origin residing in the higher hills. The third and much smaller group constituted a number of tribal communities, such as the Tharus and the Dhimals of the Terai; they were remnants of indigenous communities whose inhabitancy precedes the advent of early migration of the Indo-Nepali and Tibeto-Mongols.[15]

Despite the fact that the Indo-Nepali migrants were late comers to Nepal, relative to the migrants from the north, they dominated Nepal numerically, socially, politically, and economically. They achieved dominance over the native and northern migrant populations, for the most part; due to the superior formal educational and technological systems they brought in with them and as a result dominated the ethnic society.[16]

Amongst the Indo-Nepali group, at least two distinct categories existed. The first category comprised those who had fled India and moved to the safe sanctuaries of the Nepal hills in the wake of the Muslim invasions of northern India. The hill group of Indian origin primarily was framed of descendants of high-caste Hindu families. This section of the Indo-Nepali population also consisted of Nepal's erstwhile royal family. Other ethnic groups, along with those of Indian origins that settled in the Terai, have been peripheral to the existing governmental hierarchy.

Nepali or *Khas Kura* was the language of the Paharis and is considered the national language of Nepal; it is closely related to Hindi. Both have their roots in Sanskrit. The Hindu culture of the Pahari people has been also influenced by Buddhism and indigenous folklore. Likewise, the Bhote or Bhotia groups inhabiting the foothills of the Himalayas, among whom exist the Sherpas who have developed regional differentiations among themselves, although they are distinctly related both physically and culturally to the Tibetans. The term Bhote literally means inhabitant of Bhot, a Sanskrit term for the trans-Himalayan region of Nepal, or the Tibetan region. Bhote is also a generic term, often applied to people of Tibetan culture or Mongoloid physical composition.[17]

An inordinately composite terrain also touched the geographic distribution and fundamental interaction within several ethnic groups. Amongst the general classification of the Indo-Nepali and the Tibeto-Nepalese groups, there was a lateral (longitudinal) pattern, in which several ethnic populations were focused in specific geographic pockets. The existing valleys and mountains divide ethnic groups into numerous small, relatively isolated and more or less self-contained communities. This pattern was particularly true among the Tibeto-Nepali population.[18] For instance, the Bhotes were discovered far north, in the trans-Himalayan division of the mountain region, close to the Tibetan border. The Sherpas, a subgroup within the Bhote, were centralised in the northeast, around the Mount Everest region. To the south of this region were other Tibeto-Nepali ethnic groups, like the Gurungs in the west-middle hills and the Tamang and Rai in the east-middle hills, especially close to and east of the Kathmandu Valley. The Magar group live in the central middle hills and are more widely distributed than the Gurung, the Tamang, and the Rai. In the east, the middle hills are populated by the Limbu and Rai people, the Limbu a little farther east outside the Rai zone. The Tharus are settled in the Terai, and the Paharis are scattered throughout Nepal. Newars are mostly concentrated in the Kathmandu Valley. Nonetheless, due to their earlier migration as traders and merchants from India, who further migrated to almost all the market centres, as also as far-off as Lhasa.

Relationship with the British Empire

The British Empire requested Nepal for help in 1857-58 during India's first war of Independence. To curry favour with the British, Nepal's Prime Minister and Commander-in-chief, Jung Bahadur Rana, himself, took part in the quelling of the independence movement, along with some 17,000 Nepalese troops. In the process, about 5,000 freedom fighters were killed and approximately 500 captured in various Indian towns by the Nepalese expedition as a result of which their relations with the British improved.[19] On 18 November 1860, an agreement between the two governments was signed ceding the plains between the Mahakali and Rapti rivers, known as the Terai region to Nepal. This had been lost by Nepal in the 1816 Sugauli Treaty and returned by the grateful British; it has remained with Nepal ever since.[20]

During the First World War (WWI), the Maharaja of Nepal declared that all the military resources of Nepal are at His Majesty's disposal and shall be proud to be of any service, however little it may be.[21] Almost two million Gorkhas have fought for Britain, coming to be known as Gurkhas in the Indian Army. Twenty years later another serious crisis occurred, which saw the Gorkhas fight in greater numbers than in any other previous campaign in their history. However, the question remained, how did the once renowned imperial soldiers of the empire, successfully maintain their reputation of being brave, loyal, and formidable fighting soldiers dedicated to the British Raj in the Second World War (WWII)?

The post-WWI legislation primarily assigned the Indian Army only for the defence of India against external aggression and the maintenance of internal peace and tranquillity.[22] As suggested by this legislation, the

Gorkhas remained extremely active for two primary tasks of the Indian Army; firstly, as an imperial defence, and secondly as an internal security force. Many historians claim that fighting in the North West Frontier (NWF) during the inter-war period proved to be a training ground for the Gorkhas. However, it is important to understand to what extent fighting irregular warfare helped in dealing with the ever-evolving methods of war. Despite India's immense contribution in WWI, it was viewed as less of a priority at the start of WWII; The external role of the Indian Army during the war was limited to providing a few brigades of reinforcements in Egypt and Malaya,[23] as an imperial reserve. Instead, London ordered GHQ India (General Headquarters India) to continue to retain its inter-war role as a primary task. Research has shown that many GHQ senior commanders had traditionalist views regarding the modernisation of the Indian Army. The old unenthusiastic behaviour of London coupled with a traditionalist practice resulted in the Indian Army being ill-prepared for war. Despite many years of soldiering on harsh frontiers, the mobilisation of the Gorkhas for war came much later than the rest of the Indian Army. The war and mobilisation offered an opportunity to end the old system of Indianization. However, it barely affected the Gurkha Brigade, as it continued to be a unique organisation, within the Imperial Indian Army.

Initially, the Gorkhas enjoyed relative success against an inferior enemy in the Middle East; however, post a series of defeats in North Africa, it became clear that these tough and hardy Gorkha soldiers were not trained for the kind of desert warfare that they were being made to fight. Further, as was the practice and the thought process prevailing at that time, senior British officers continued to grossly underestimate the performance of the Indian Army including the Gurkha regiments. However, the victory of the 4th Indian Division in Tunisia proved to be a turning point that forced them to re-evaluate this erroneous assessment.

As a result, the Gorkhas fought other significant battles as specialist regiments in the re-conquest and liberation of Europe. Nevertheless, these successes in the Middle East and North Africa were overshadowed by the series of humiliating defeats in the Far East. The creation of the Japanese-sponsored Indian National Army (INA), after the fall of Singapore that supported the ongoing Quit India movement, created considerable strains on the performance of the Brigade of the Gorkhas at a time of reformation for the Indian Army. The renewed loyalty of the Gurkhas was tested critically at this juncture. Significantly, it was against the Japanese in Burma that the Gorkhas showed their supreme superiority against the enemy, more than in any other theatre of war.

The Japanese defeat in the Second Arakan Offensive and with the successes of the Chindits operations confirmed, it soon became clear that the Japanese were not the "Gods of the Jungle." The previous criticism towards the Gorkhas performance in the First Chindits was overshadowed by their superb performance in the second operation. Also, the desperate Japanese offensive in 1944 had been halted by the superior fighting qualities performed by the Gorkhas, which finally led to the fall of Burma into British hands.

The Royal Nepalese Army (RNA) in its entirety took part in the First World War and the total number of Nepalese troops deployed in India at the time was approximately 14,000 soldiers. Subsequently, both in 1917 and 1919, the RNA was involved in the suppression of freedom movements both in Waziristan and Afghanistan. Later, following a bilateral treaty, 17 infantry units and several high-ranking Nepalese officers participated in the WWII. When Japan jumped into this war in December 1940 and the British existence was threatened in the Indian subcontinent, the RNA was positioned in India and on the Burma front, where it fought with great courage under the 14th Army under General William Slim, helping turn defeat into victory and ultimately a Japanese retreat.

Geographical Location

India and Nepal have a long-lasting heritage of a shared history since recorded time. This is facilitated to a great deal by the geographical proximity of these nations. Nepal lies along the mountains of the central portion of the Himalayas. The land slopes downwards from the almost impenetrable and mighty Himalayan wall of the north until it reaches the southern fertile Terai plains of the Ganges in south; central hill region with rugged Himalayas in north. The narrow track of the Terai plains was once covered by thick tropical forests known as the Char Kose Jhadi or malarial curtain.[24] Most of the population is divided nearly equally between a concentration in the southern-most plains of the Terai region and the central hilly region; overall density is quite low. India lies to the south of the Terai. The river Mechi, which flows between the eastern boundary of Nepal and India, formed the eastern border and the river Mahakali in Western Nepal became the western border of Nepal.[25]

The Nepal Himalayas consist of four major massifs – Nanda Devi (25,700 feet), Dhaulagiri (26,826 feet), Gosainthan (26,305 feet) and Kanchenjunga (28,156 feet) – making the formidable northern wall throughout the length of the country. The 29,028-foot Mount Everest lies roughly midway and gives off no main ridges.[26]

Nepal's shape is roughly rectangular, about 650 kilometres long and about 200 kilometres wide, comprising a total of 147,181 square kilometres of land. Nepal is located in southern Asia, between China and India. It has a total land boundary of 3,159 kilometres and its bordering countries, China has 1,389 kilometres, and India has 1,770 kilometres. The landlocked country contains eight of the world's 10 highest peaks, including Mount Everest and Kanchenjunga – the world's highest and third tallest mountain – on the borders with China and India, respectively.[27]

A landlocked country, it is surrounded by India on three sides and by China's Xizang Autonomous Region (Tibet) to the north. It is separated from Bangladesh by an approximately 15-kilometre wide strip of India's West Bengal state, and from Bhutan by the 88-kilometre wide Sikkim state, also of India. Nepal is almost totally dependent on India for transit facilities and access to the sea, that is, the Bay of Bengal.[28]

Geographical position and historical development are largely determining factors of Nepal's foreign policy that regardless of the kaleidoscopic change of contemporary events and no matter what form of government has been instituted or what political party may be in power, it has a natural tendency to return again and again to the same general and fundamental alignment.[29] This is applicable in the Indo-Nepalese context and has been evident in political relations since the establishment of the modern state of Nepal from its inception to the current period.

This unique location of Nepal is of immense strategic value to India as well as to China. India has traditionally looked at its northern frontiers with China as the Himalayan watershed. The Himalayan watershed forms a formidable military barrier that can be crossed at selected places only and therefore lends itself for a strong defence line requiring significantly lesser resources to defend. Any Chinese military or ideological influx or influence south of this watershed would be inimical to Indian interests and since the mountains of Nepal open out to the great Indian plains, it becomes crucial to safeguard the military interests of India.

China, on the other hand, views its borders with Nepal as the soft underbelly of Tibet.[30] It, therefore, finds it necessary to ensure that it retains adequate political, strategic, and economic leverage in Nepal so that its security is not compromised.

The China-Nepal boundary extends for 670 miles along the crest of the Himalaya Mountains. The present boundary was established as a result of the boundary agreement signed between Nepal and China on 21 March 1960. A joint boundary commission subsequently delimited and formally demarcated the boundary. There are 96 boundary pillars bearing 76 serial numbers over the entire boundary. The frontier region is dominated by the vast mountain ranges of the Himalayas. In the south, the zone of the Sub- or Outer-Himalaya comprises a series of narrow, parallel ridges alternating with broad, longitudinal valleys. The peaks of this group rarely exceed 4,000 feet in elevation. Northward are the Middle Ranges of the Himalayas, which have a steep escarpment to the south and moderate slopes towards the north. In this group, peaks are between 5,000 and 15,000 feet in elevation. Beyond is the Inner or Greater Himalaya, a complex region of young, folded mountains, interrupted by faults and overthrusts. The main ranges are aligned generally west-northwest-east-southeast. Elevations range from 14,000 feet to over 29,000 feet in the great majesty of Mount Everest (Chomolungma; Sagarmatha). The China-Nepal boundary traverses the Great Himalaya Range, the highest mountain ranges in the world. Jagged peaks, capped for the most part in perpetual snow, rise above towering ridge lines. Five peaks – Everest, Kanchenjunga, Makalu, Dhaulagiri, and Annapurna, attain heights above 26,400 feet while most of the region exceeds 14,000 feet. Even the principal passes through the border range are almost all over 16,000 feet in elevation. The many rivers and streams have cut steep ravine-like valleys through the Great Himalayan ranges. Tributaries of the Karnali, Kali, Kosi, and Arun rivers drain, in fact, the Tibetan slopes before turning south to cut through the ranges in deep gorges to flow to the Ganges. North of the boundary ranges stretches the high Tibetan plateau. Here the nearly-level rock formations, averaging about 15,000 feet in elevation, dip gently northward to the valley of the Tsang Po (Brahmaputra).

Similarly, there are a number of passes connecting Nepal with Tibet, such as the Takla Khar Pass, the Mustang Pass and the Kuti Pass, but it is extremely hard for Nepal to gain access to the sea via Tibetan territories to Chinese ports. The Kodari Highway links Nepal with Tibet in the north and currently, with Chinese assistance the Rasuwa-Syaphrubesi road is being constructed. After the completion of the Rasuwa-Syaphrubesi road, it will be the second road link to Tibet. Nepal and China have reached an understanding to open up other links such as in Mustang, Kimathanka–Sankhuwasabha and Humla. If these proposed links are opened, the flow of Nepal-China trade, tourism as well as other economic and cultural activities like in the past would be enhanced further bringing the populations of Nepal and China closer. The Siliguri corridor, the only rail and road link between the rest of India and its north-eastern states, also merits serious consideration. Its security is, therefore, vital for India, and can be jeopardised by a small military manoeuvre or by subverting the people living in this area. Subversion can be easily carried out by political or ideological or religious fundamentalist forces both in Nepal and in Bangladesh. Chinese military presence south of the watershed will pose serious threats to this area.[31]

Nepal's southern borders with India do not have geographical barriers and are open, porous and in places difficult to monitor by security personnel. Any anti-India activity in Nepalese border areas will find easy access to a poorly guarded and insecure Indian heartland. These activities could be Pakistan's Inter-Services Intelligence (ISI)-sponsored violence, smuggling, drug running, and other economic offences.

All the rivers, namely, Budhi Ganga, Karnali, Andhikhola, Kali Gandaki, Dudh Koshi, Kabeli, and the like, originating or flowing in Nepal merge into the Ganga River. Unchecked flows every year cause floods leading to serious social and economic havoc in India. Nepal plans to construct storage dams as well as electricity generation plants for its domestic demand and accordingly, the Nationwide Master Plan Study on Storage-type Hydroelectric Power Development in Nepal (2011-2014) was undertaken to prepare a power development plan for 20 years from 2013 and to select promising storage-type hydroelectric power projects from 65 potential projects listed in the long list prepared by the Nepal Electricity Authority (NEA), taking into account technical, environmental, economic and financial issues. The development scale of these promising projects was proposed to be about 100 MW to 300 MW.[32] Any uncontrolled release of water during critical periods of the monsoons may be detrimental to India's security requirements. A close and friendly relationship is therefore warranted as any inimical political setup may be unresponsive to India's concerns and release of water at critical moments during the monsoon period will have very serious consequences, economically and socially, for India.

A large number of other issues such as trade, transit and investment relations are also included in the strategic importance of Nepal.

Water resources are considered the backbone of Nepali economy. The issue of water resources has always been getting due prominence in the agenda of bilateral cooperation between Nepal and India for a long time. To optimize benefits and address the problems, both governments have set up three-tier mechanisms called Joint Ministerial Commission for Water Resources (JMCWR), Joint Committee on Water Resources (JCWR) and Joint Standing Technical Committee (JSTC) to implement agreements and treaties and also address water-induced problems of flood and inundation.[33]

Security related issues are of prime concern to both the countries. To deal jointly with each other's security concerns, the two countries have institutionalized Home Secretary-level meetings and established Joint Working Group (JWG) on Border Management and Border District Coordination Committees (BDCCs).[34]

Both Nepal and India have a common approach to regional and multilateral institutions, and hence, work in tandem in the United Nations, Non-aligned Movement and other international forums on most of the important international issues. Furthermore, both the countries have been deeply engaged in the regional and sub-regional frameworks of the South Asian Association for Regional Cooperation (SAARC), Bay of Bengal Initiative for Multi-Sectoral Technical and Economic Cooperation (BIMSTEC) and the Bangladesh, Bhutan, India, Nepal Initiative (BBIN) for enhancing cooperation for greater economic integration by collectively harnessing the potentials and complementarities available in the region.[35]

India and Nepal share common and interdependent economic cultural and social links. Both are democracies and retention of this political state of affairs is highly desirable.

India's Security Concerns

India, keeping in mind Nepal's topographical similarities and contiguity, is of the opinion that militarily the mountains of Nepal open out to the great Indian plains where defensible lines will be difficult to establish and, therefore, finds it necessary to ensure that it retains adequate political, strategic and economic leverage in Nepal so that its security is not compromised. Nepal is always considered part of its northern security system. It, therefore, expects Nepal to remain sensitive to its security concerns. This expectation of India has been misinterpreted in Nepal as an attack on Nepal's sovereignty and independence, especially since Nepal feels vulnerable in case of any external powers presence on Nepalese territory beyond normal diplomatic activity. On the other hand, Nepal is also fully aware that India could take care of its economic development and security concerns more effectively than any other country including China. This feeling of interdependency has been reflected in the 1950 Treaty and also during official visits.

Indo-Nepal relations have remained responsive to changing dynamics of strategic environment built on more friendly terms. Nepal lies in the southern lap of the Himalayas, and shares borders with two large states of Asia. This geopolitical reality has to be taken into account.

Nepal and India enjoy excellent bilateral ties. Founded on the age-old connection of history, culture, tradition, and religion, these relations are close, comprehensive, and multidimensional and are pronounced more in political, social, cultural, religious, and economic engagements with each other. To add formal flavour to such historic relations, the two countries established diplomatic relations on 17 June 1947. The unwavering commitment to the principles of peaceful coexistence, sovereign equality, and understanding of each other's aspirations and sensitivities has been the firm foundation on which our bilateral relations have been growing further. The open border between the two countries remains a unique feature of our relations. A frontier without restriction has greatly facilitated the free movement of our people to each other's territory and enhanced interactions.[36]

China's role in Nepal has expanded steadily over the last decades. To counter China's reach in Nepal, India must act speedily and steadily to improve its weak overland infrastructure in the Himalayas. India must improve its diplomacy vis-à-vis Nepal and show greater benevolence and flexibility towards it. Nepal and India will gain if they establish bridges of opportunities rather than mistrusting each other.

Unfortunately limited work that has been done until now to analyse and understand the role of external powers, as well as their influence on Nepalese politics and foreign policy, especially in post-monarchy period. In addition, there has been no attempt to understand the extremely positive role that the Indian Army and its vast network of veterans, pensioners, and serving soldiers can play in changing existing mindsets and conflict areas. Therefore, in this book, an attempt is being made to both comprehend the strategic interests of its entrenched elite living in Kathmandu, China, the USA, India, the EU and major European countries and Pakistan as well as incorporate in our outreach the Indian Army's ability to significantly and positively alter existing adverse mindsets.

NOTES

1. DESA, UN. United Nations Department of Economic and Social Affairs/Statistics Division, Population and Vital Statistics Report. Statistical Papers Series A, vol. LXVIII, 2016, p. 4.

2. Bose, S. & Jalal, A. *Modern South Asia: history, culture, political economy,* Psychology Press, Delhi, 2004, p. 4.
3. Daniels, P. T. & Bright, W. (eds.), *The worlds writing systems*, Oxford University Press, London, 1996, pp. 564-568.
4. Rai, B. *Gorkhas: The Warrior Race*, Kalpaz Publications, Delhi, 2009, p. 103.
5. Jayasundara, N. S, The development of language education policy: An Indian Perspective; a view from Tamil Nadu, *International Journal of Scientific and Research Publications*, vol. 4, issue 11, 2014, pp. 1-2.
6. Bose, S. & Jalal, A, op. cit., p. 4.
7. Stiller, L F. *The rise of the house of Gorkha: a study in the unification of Nepal, 1768-1816,* Manjusri Pub. House, New Delhi, 1973, p. 1.
8. Rai, B. op. cit., p. 7.
9. Ibid.
10. Rai, B. op. cit., p. 3.
11. Stiller, L. F. op. cit., p. 8.
12. Sanjay Upadhya (ed.), *Nepal and the Geo-Strategic Rivalry between China and India*, Routledge Studies in South Asian Politics), 1st edn., Kindle Edition, 1991, pp. 24-25.
13. Rai, B. *Gorkhas: The Warrior Race,* Kalpaz Publications, Delhi, 2009, p. 9.
14. Ibid.
15. Ibid.
16. Ibid.
17. Ibid.
18. Rai, B. op. cit., p. 11.
19. Nepalese Army - Official Site. http://www.nepalarmy.mil.np/ accessed 25 November 2015.
20. Ibid.
21. Smith, E. D. *Britains Brigade of Gurkhas*, Leo Cooper Ltd., 1973, London, p. 84.
22. Elliott, Maj-Gen. J.G. *A roll of Honour, The story of the Indian Army 1939-1945*, Cassell and Company Ltd., 1965, London, p. 13.
23. Gould. T. *Imperial Warriors: Britain and the Gurkhas*, Granta Books, 1999, London, p. 236.
24. Lal, C.K. Political ecology of the madhes, *Nepali Times*, August-September 2017 at www.nepalitimes com/issue/364/ State of the State /13907 accessed 14 September 2015.
25. Gerung, H, Nepali Nationalism, Telegraph Nepal, 26 August 2010 at http:// www.telegraphnepal.com/news_det. php? news_id=2080 accessed 14 September 2015.
26. Ibid.
27. Central Intelligence Agency (CIA), *The World Factbook*, https://www.cia.gov/library/ publications/the-world-factbook/geos/np.html
28. http://www.nepalmountainnews.com/cms/about-nepal/geography accessed 14 September 2014.
29. Chamberlain, A.; Cambon, J; von Kühlmann, R.; & Davis, J. W. The Permanent Bases of German Foreign Policy, *Foreign Affairs* (An American Quarterly Review), vol. 9, issue 2, 1931, pp. 179-194.
30. Adhikary, D. Political impasse takes Nepal to brink, *Asia Times*, 17 November 2009 at http://yubabahas.com/?p=20795 accessed 12 March 2016.
31. Verma, B. Nightmare 2012: Chinese Special Forces cut off Siliguri corridor, *Indian Defence Review*, vol. 25, issue: 2, April-June, 2010, p. 27.

32. Nepal Electricity Authority (NEA), Nationwide Master Plan Study on Storage-type Hydroelectric Power Development in Nepal: Final Report Summary, Japan International Cooperation Agency Electric Power Development Co., Ltd., Nepal, February 2014, pp. annex 2/2.
33. Ministry of Foreign Affairs, Nepal-India Relations, https://mofa.gov.np/nepal-india-relations/#: ~:text=Nepal%2DIndia%20relations%20are%2C%20in, ties%20between %20the%20two%20countries
34. Ibid.
35. Ibid.
36. Ibid.

1

INDIA-NEPAL BILATERAL RELATIONS POST-INDEPENDENCE UNDER THE GROWING CHINESE PRESENCE

Introduction

The relationship between India and Nepal has been historically complex and influenced by various factors, including geopolitical considerations, cultural ties, and economic interests. The presence of China in Nepal has added another dimension to this relationship.

China's increasing influence in Nepal has been a matter of concern for India, as it has implications for regional geopolitics. The Belt and Road Initiative (BRI), a massive infrastructure and connectivity project led by China, has seen Nepal participate in certain projects. This has led to increased economic and strategic ties between China and Nepal.

The India-Nepal relationship faced some challenges in recent times, including border disputes and issues related to the new political map released by Nepal that incorporated territories disputed with India. These disputes led to tensions between the two countries. Additionally, Nepal has sought to diversify its international partnerships, including strengthening ties with China. The foreign policy of India or any country is shaped by two factors – domestic and international. Domestically, India's history, culture, geography and economy have played an important role in determining the objectives and principles of India's foreign policy. Under domestic factors, the role of geographical, historical, economic and cultural circumstances needs to be understood. Geographically, India is surrounded by the Indian Ocean on three sides, the Himalayas in the north, great desert in the west and hilly terrain in the north-east. The international factor, characterized by Cold War rivalry between the North Atlantic Treaty Organization (NATO) and the Warsaw Pact, the establishment of the United Nations, arms race, particularly nuclear arms race, anti-colonialism and anti-imperialism, and the like have also influenced the priorities and objectives of our foreign policy.

That said, foreign policy is not a static concept as it keeps on changing as per domestic and international politics. National security is an example of one of these core principles. The foreign policy of independent and democratic India was a clean departure from that of the colonial power that had adopted the policy of bringing other states under its rule by the use of force or intrigue.

India adopted the policy of helping democratic movements in its neighbourhood. It had supported Nepal's democratic movement which overthrew the century-long Rana family rule, reinstalling King Tribhuvan on the throne and ushered in democratic polity.[1] Post-independence, the special relationship between India and Nepal started with the India-Nepal Treaty of Peace and Friendship in 1950 and accompanying letters that defined security relations between the two countries as well as an agreement governing both bilateral trade and trade transiting Indian soil.

Evolution of Nepal's Foreign Policy

As a small and landlocked country, Nepal's foreign policy priorities were to preserve and protect its territorial integrity from its neighbours.[2] During the Panchayat regime which was the political system of Nepal from 1960 to 1990 based on the panchayat system of self-governance, any threat to the monarchy was considered as a threat to the sovereignty of the country and vice-versa. Thus, the survival of the monarchy became synonymous with state security.[3] As a result, Nepal's foreign policy was designed to protect its territorial integrity by maintaining a balance between India and

China, adherence to the UN principles and being part of regional organizations. Its foreign policy was also specially formulated to mobilise international support and recognition with the purpose of fulfilling its political and economic requirements.[4] Articulating Nepal's foreign policy priorities, in view of its geographic reality, King Prithvi Narayan Shah said that Nepal was like a yam between two boulders, and should maintain an equal relationship with China (then Tibet) and India. S.D. Muni, in 1973 observed that the foreign policy objectives of small states like Nepal are motivated by security (territorial integrity and military), stability (political and economic), and status, but these motivations may not be enough to decipher Nepal's foreign policy. Therefore, it is important to examine some structural factors that influence such policies. The structural factors may be constant (e.g., geography, history, socio-cultural ties with its larger neighbour) or variable (e.g., nationalism and political system).[5] To fulfil its foreign policy objectives, Nepal adopted the strategy of, firstly, taking advantage of the differences and clash of interests between India and China; secondly, reducing dependence on both neighbours by diversifying its foreign relations; and thirdly, mobilisation of international contacts for building counter-pressures.[6]

Absolute Monarchy (1950-1970)

The period 1951-1955 under King Tribhuvan sowed the seeds for future Nepalese disenchantment with India. With the Indo-Nepal Treaty of Peace and Friendship signed between the two countries in 1950, bilateral relations between the nations improved. Nepal welcomed close relations with India but as the number of Nepalese living and working in India increased and the involvement of India in Nepal's economy deepened, so too did Nepalese discomfort with this special relationship. Tensions came to a head in the mid-1970s, when Nepal pressed for substantial amendments in its favour in the trade and transit treaty and openly criticized India's 1975 annexation of Sikkim which it considered as part of Greater Nepal. In 1975, when King Birendra proposed that Nepal be recognised internationally as a zone of peace, he received support from China and Pakistan; however, in India's view, this proposal by the King was unnecessary and a repudiation of the existing special relationship fostered by the 1950 Peace and Friendship

Treaty. In many ways, this also represented a possible threat to India's security and therefore could not be endorsed. However, Nepal continually promoted this proposal in all international forums with Chinese support.[7]

In 1950, the Indo-Nepal Treaty of Peace and Friendship was signed between the two countries; however, there have been anti-India protests in Nepal against India's overbearing attitude and perceived interference in its internal affairs over the years. These crystallised into widespread anti-India sentiments.[8] Almost every section of the people especially the educated elite of Kathmandu and courtiers of the King sought in China, a much-needed counter-weight against India. This could also be directly attributable to Nepal's asymmetry in size, psychology, and continuing poverty.

Another issue that was continually being raised was the induction of the Indian Military Mission (IMM) in 1952 along with Indian technicians to man 17 check points on the Sino-Nepalese border. This was done to ostensibly monitor Chinese signal communications, with US signal equipment in 1954.

With King Mahindra's rise to power in March 1955, Nepal articulated a new balance of power policy in relation to its neighbours, which was fundamentally different from the existing policy of special relations with India. This balance of power policy had three main features:

(a) Extension and maintenance of friendship based on mutual respect and goodwill, with every one of its neighbours;
(b) Exploitation of regional differences between neighbours to further self-interests;
(c) Declared stand of neutrality in the disputes between its neighbours.[9]

In July 1955, China and Nepal established diplomatic relations based on the principles of Panchsheel. This was followed in December 1955 by its admission to the UN as a full-fledged member. In March 1960, China and Nepal signed an Agreement of Peace and Friendship. In 1962, Nepal and Pakistan signed the protocol for instituting full diplomatic relations.[10] This was the beginning of the outward thrust by Nepal, an international outlook that saw little advantage in clinging to regional alignments. Further, Indian continual support to democratic and pro-Congress elements in Nepal and its perceived overbearing attitude had alienated King Mahendra considerably. He dismissed the parliamentary system of democracy in December 1960 and strengthened his relations with China at India's expense. By October 1962, a few days prior to the Sino-Indian war, King Mahendra had returned from a visit to Beijing where the vice PM assured him that if any forces attacked Nepal, the Chinese people would stand by it.[11] A year earlier, in October 1961, both countries had signed the Boundary Treaty by which Nepal gained some 300 square miles of territory.

There was little doubt that Nepalese leanings towards China were at a tilt, historically validated as a balance of power gambit. The Indian defeat in the 1962 war against China marked a significant change in the attitude of Nepal towards India and China. The main concern in Kathmandu was that a powerful China posed, possibly, a much larger threat to Nepal than India could militarily. Also, if India could not protect itself, how could they expect India to protect Nepal?

The intrinsic strengths of China in the north and India in the south were not lost on the policy makers of Nepal and this was borne out by the advice of Prithvi Narayan Shah to his successors, the kingdom is like a yam between two boulders. Maintain friendly relations with the Emperor of China; great friendship should also be maintained with the emperor beyond the southern seas.[12] This balance has continued since.

Indian Economic Blockade of Nepal (1989-1990)

Nepal is among the least developed countries in the world, with about one-quarter of its population living below the poverty line. Nepal is heavily dependent on remittances, which amount to as much as 30 per cent of the GDP. Agriculture is the mainstay of the economy, providing a livelihood for almost two-thirds of the population but accounting for less than a third of the GDP. Industrial activity mainly involves the processing of agricultural products, including pulses, jute, sugarcane, tobacco, and grain.[13]

In 1978, India agreed to separate trade and transit treaties, satisfying a long-term Nepalese demand. In 1988, when the two treaties were up for renewal, Nepal's refusal to accommodate India's wishes on the transit treaty caused India to call for a single trade and transit treaty. Thereafter, Nepal took a hard-line position that led to a serious crisis in India-Nepal relations. After two extensions, the two treaties expired on 23 March 1989, resulting in a virtual Indian economic blockade of Nepal that lasted until late April 1990. Although economic issues were a major factor in the two countries confrontation, Indian dissatisfaction with Nepal's 1988 acquisition of Chinese weaponry had also played an important role.

Treaties and letters exchanged in 1959 and 1965 included Nepal in India's security zone and precluded arms purchases without India's approval. India linked security with economic relations and insisted on reviewing India-Nepal relations as a whole. Nepal had to back down after worsening economic conditions led to a change in Nepal's political system in which the King was forced to re-institute parliamentary democracy. The new government sought quick restoration of amicable relations with India.[14]

Indo-Nepal Bilateral Relations (1990-2000)

By 1990, Indian intelligence agencies had discovered that Kathmandu had emerged as an important outpost of the ISI. Nepal itself had acknowledged the ISIs growing presence through the expulsion of Pakistani diplomats from its soil. It had also, in its parleys with India, accepted the ISIs penetration and even sought help for dealing with the menace. For most part, Nepal had pleaded its helplessness in checking the ISI's activities.[15] This development along with the large-scale narcotics trade and smuggling through the porous border had emerged as very potent threats to India's security. These issues need in-depth analysis and counter-measures, while ensuring that bilateral relations do not suffer beyond acceptable limits. These fault lines will be covered later in this book.

The special security relationship between New Delhi and Kathmandu was re-established in June 1990, post the New Delhi meeting of Nepal's Prime Minister, Krishna Prasad Bhattarai and the Indian Prime Minister, V.P. Singh. During the December 1991 visit to India by Nepalese Prime Minister Girija Prasad Koirala, the two countries signed new, separate trade and transit treaties and other economic agreements designed to accord Nepal's additional economic benefits.

Indian-Nepali relations appeared to be undergoing still more reassessment when Nepal's Prime Minister Man Mohan Adhikary visited New Delhi in April 1995 and insisted on a major review of the 1950 peace and friendship treaty. In the face of benign statements by his Indian hosts relating to the treaty, Adhikary sought greater economic independence for his landlocked nation while simultaneously striving to improve ties with China.

The period from 1960 to 2000 saw a series of highs and lows in India-Nepal bilateral relations. In the 1970s, Nepal pressed for substantial amendments in its favour in the trade and transit treaty and openly criticized Sikkim's merger with India, which it considered as part of Greater Nepal. India sponsored Nepal's admission to the United Nations (UN) Organization in 1990. Bilateral relations with India got a further boost with an agreement to resume water talks after a four-year hiatus.[16]

The Political Scenario

Nepal-India relations are, in essence, much more than the sum of treaties and agreements concluded between the two countries. The frequent high-level visits by the leaders of the two countries at different points of time and the interactions constitute the hallmark of the ties between the two countries. Furthermore, such visits have helped promote goodwill, trust, understanding and cooperation between the two countries and, have injected fresh momentum to further consolidate age-old and multi-faceted bilateral relations of friendship and cooperation on a more mature and pragmatic footing.[17]

The unfathomable commitment to the principles of peaceful coexistence, sovereign equality and understanding of each other's aspirations and interests remain the firm foundations of any bilateral relations. The open border between the two countries has been a unique paradigm of the political and geographical ties that rarely exist around the world. Keeping India's vulnerabilities with regard to cross-border terrorism, Nepal was expected not to allow its territory to be misused by any inimical elements against India and also expected similar reciprocity and assurances from India.

Diplomatic Cooperation and Multilateral Forums

Both countries had displayed similarity of purpose and had worked together in various international forums like the UN, Non-aligned Movement (NAM) and others. SAARC and BIMSTEC in South Asia opened up more avenues for enhancing regional cooperation and were identified for further improvement in that direction.

Nepal has, on many occasions, successfully utilised multilateral forums and the UN to neutralise and minimise the influence of neighbouring countries in its internal matters. For example, Nepal was a founding member of both the NAM and SAARC. In both these multilateral arrangements, Nepal has successfully raised the concerns of small states and has sought to establish that it is not influenced by any country; that being a sovereign country, it has created a space for itself at the international level.

Maoist Armed Conflict in Nepal

An insurgency led by Maoists broke out in 1996. During the ensuing 10-year civil war between Maoist and government forces, the monarchy dissolved the cabinet and Parliament and re-assumed absolute power in 2002, after the Crown Prince massacred the royal family in 2001. A peace accord in 2006 led to the promulgation of an interim constitution in 2007. Following a nationwide Constituent Assembly (CA) election in 2008, the newly formed CA declared Nepal a federal democratic republic, abolished the monarchy, and elected the country's first president.[18]

For greater detail on the Maoist insurrection in Nepal, an attempt has been made to elaborate on its causes. The Maoist conflict emerged in the initial period of democracy as the growing awareness and empowerment of the Nepalese people during the initial years of multiparty democracy was realised, especially after the 1990s political transition that established democratic politics.

Nepal was a monolithic, feudalistic, autocratic, authoritarian, centralised and closed state for centuries.[19] The state governing system in the entire history of modern Nepal was orchestrated by cajoling, threat of suppression and use of coercive power by the state.[20] Such characteristics of the state consequently excluded a vast majority of Nepalese people from the nation-building process.[21] All these led to a breeding ground of insurgency in Nepal. Rampant poverty, abject destitution, systematic and deliberate exclusion; severe caste, gender, and ethnic discrimination; and greater injustice have been identified by many researchers and analysts as structural causes of the ongoing armed conflict.[22]

Babu Ram Bhattarai, senior leader of the Maoists, has vividly explained his perspective on the socio-political structures of society as the core of the problem of Nepal, which is acknowledged in the theoretical documents of the Maoists.[23] According to the Maoists, the principal objective of the People's War was to develop the social productive forces and create a higher form of society through a continuous revolution ... by putting politics in command.[24] Therefore, the Maoists argue that they are not the problem but the solution of the problem facing the nation for a long time.

There have been over the past decade several unanswered questions on the following issues:

(a) How and why did this Maoist insurgency emerge?
(b) Why the past two negotiations had failed?
(c) Why did the King opt for the 1 February coup?
(d) What are the initiatives taken so far by political parties, civil society, and media in resolving this crisis and what are the opportunities for conflict transformation?

For all those questions, the answers are generic and have yet to be fully studied by either the government or the academia. Some of the generic issues could be lack of governance or its absolute failure, lack of development and its failure, the failure or inability of the Royal Palace to understand and respond to the grievances of subjects and that the ill-advised February 1 royal takeover, the ideological dimension of the spread of communism and its ideological cousin the Maoists, and the failure of the existing constitution be sensitive to its citizenry and their growing aspirations.

Since the end of the centuries-old monarchy in Nepal in 2008, the country has seen 10 governments. The chief reason for the frequent change in the country's leadership is political factionalism. In 2018, after the communist parties joined hands to form a coalition government, many political observers strongly believed that the coalition would complete its five-year term. However, this did not happen. Leadership issues broke the communist alliance. The Communist Party of Nepal (Maoist Centre) or CPN (Maoist Centre), withdrew from the government, led by K.P. Sharma Oli, and extended its support to the Nepali Congress (NC) which formed the next coalition government in July 2021. In the recent elections in November 2022, the CPN (Maoist Centre) contested as a part of the NC-led coalition. However, after the announcement of the electoral results, the CPN (Maoist Centre) again switched sides to lead a coalition government. Notably, the NC is the largest single party with 89 members in the House of Representatives while the CPN (Maoist Centre) only has 32 members. Given the past political equations between the leaders Pushpa Kamal Dahal alias Prachanda and Oli, a question on political stability remains.

The post-1990 governance failure provided the space for conflict escalation because of:

(a) Its inability to fulfil people's expectations, degenerating into misgovernance, and
(b) The freedom it offered. Consequently, people widely supported the democratic movement of 1990 and multiparty democracy was restored.[25]

Governance failure, development failure, dissatisfaction of the palace, ideological dimension, and constitutional dimension all led the nation to raise their voice against injustice, poverty and social exclusion. People became more aware about poverty, inequality, discrimination, corruption and lack of employment opportunities. The Constitution of the Kingdom of Nepal 1990 had opened windows of opportunities to entertain the rights of Nepalese citizens. From the 1990 popular movement, the Nepalese people moved from a closed hierarchical society to an open democratic society. This 1990 movement also raised unrealistically high expectations of the people when the political parties in the early 1990s irrationally fuelled these expectations to win the popular vote. At the same time, the state failed to address their concerns and meet their expectations.[26]

When the Maoist movement started in 1996, they submitted a 40-

point demand to the government.[27] The government could not fulfil the demands due to the three major demands that were directly related to India. These included:

(a) All discriminatory treaties, including the 1950 Nepal-India Treaty, should be abrogated;
(b) The so-called Integrated Mahakali Treaty concluded on 29 January 1996 should be repealed immediately, as it is designed to conceal the disastrous Tanakpur Treaty and allows Indian imperialist monopoly over Nepal's water resources;
(c) The open border between Nepal and India should be regulated, controlled and systematised. All vehicles with Indian licence plates should be banned from Nepal.[28]

There were major changes in Nepal's foreign policy outlook since the Maoists assumed power in August 2008. The Federal Democratic Republic of Nepal has emphasized independence in the conduct of its foreign policy. The Maoist government re-defined their policy of equidistance as a policy of non-alignment and neutrality. The practical application of this was that instead of feeding the people of Humla, a food-deficit district of Nepal, with Indian rice transported by helicopter from Nepalganj, the government would get rice from the nearby markets of Tibet.[29] Consequently, they received considerable food aid. This is a particularly important strategic move because the Humla district of Nepal is a gateway to the globally significant Kailash-Mansarovar sacred monuments located in Pulan county of the Tibet Autonomous Region of China and an important point of intersection between the cultural, environmental, economic and political features of the three nations of China, India and Nepal.[30]

Prachanda, the then prime minister, visited Beijing in August 2008 to attend the concluding ceremony of the Olympic Games. In April 2009, China proposed a revised Peace and Friendship Treaty with Nepal to improve its own standing in that country. The proposal, however, did not materialize because of the cancellation of Prachanda's visit, which was scheduled in May 2009.

Earlier, China was more focused on the Tibet issue, but it diversified its interests in Nepal after the Maoists adopted the policy of maintaining equidistance between India and China. The Nepalese scholar, P. Basnet has observed:

> "The new trend evident over the past three years (since 2008) now has China's interest in Nepal shifting from being almost exclusively focused on Tibet-related security issues (essentially preventing any Free Tibet activity out of Nepal) to being part of Beijing's larger geostrategic plan for South Asia."[31]

On the other hand, the Unified Communist Party of Nepal (Maoist) or UCPN-M, which had not abandoned its revolutionary political objective, was eager to seek China's support to counter-balance India. To oblige China, the Prachanda government took strong action against the Tibetan refugee movement in Nepal and increased border security to prevent the transit of Tibetan refugees across the border with China.

Several high-level visits were exchanged between China and the Maoist government in Nepal. These included Prime Minister Prachanda's trip to Beijing in September 2008,[32] followed by the visit of Defence Minister Ram Bahadur Thapa a few days later. China's Foreign Minister Yang Jiechi visited Nepal in December 2008. During Thapas visit in September 2008, China agreed to provide security assistance. China also agreed to provide technical assistance for the merger of the Maoist armed cadres with the Nepalese Army. China also agreed to provide economic assistance totalling NPR 1.2 billion to support Nepal's infrastructure and technical development.[33]

Like the kings of the past, the democratic governments since 2008, too sought to reduce India's influence in Nepal, with the Maoists (before the split) projecting India as an enemy state in their manifesto. The Maoist demands mentioned therein were as under:

(a) Regulated or closed border;
(b) More trade and transit facilities;
(c) Formation of Greater Nepal;
(d) Civilian nuclear units with help from China;
(e) Demarcation of borders; and
(f) Diversification of trade and free arms import.

After becoming prime minister and breaking the tradition of visiting India first, Prachanda visited Beijing to underscore Nepal's sovereignty and independence. Although he undertook his first official visit to India, his first foreign trip to Beijing[34] had indicated that the Maoists would prefer China to India. During his visit to the Nordic countries in March 2009, Prachanda articulated the view that sustainable peace was not possible in Nepal without economic prosperity and support from the international community. He requested Norway to invest in hydropower development and other sectors of mutual interest.[35] Even after his resignation, the Maoists mobilised international support to come back to power and continued to project India as an interventionist power. This Maoist policy of equidistance was also followed by the succeeding coalition government led by Madhav Kumar Nepal of the Communist Party of Nepal (Unified Marxist-Leninist) or CPN-UML, but with some moderation in policies vis-à-vis India.[36] The new prime minister, Madhav Kumar Nepal, Prime Minister of Nepal, paid an official visit to India from 18 to 22 August 2009 at the invitation of Dr. Manmohan Singh, Prime Minister of India, soon after assuming office. During the visit, the Prime Minister of Nepal stressed that bringing the peace process in Nepal to a positive and meaningful conclusion in coordination and cooperation with all concerned parties, writing a new Constitution within the stipulated time frame and accelerating the pace of economic development were the main priorities of the Government of Nepal. The two prime ministers agreed on the need to reinvigorate bilateral relations in all areas and directed that all the established institutional bilateral mechanisms should function effectively in a time-bound manner and lead to concrete outcomes for the benefit of both countries.[37]

Interestingly, his visit to Beijing in December 2009 was a high-profile one and the two countries agreed to further strengthen their relationship. China took the visit very seriously since this was the first official visit of the Nepalese prime minister to China after it became a republic. One of the longest and most detailed joint statements was issued at the end of that visit. The two countries agreed to lift their bilateral relationship to a higher level by establishing a comprehensive partnership of cooperation, which hinted at taking the relationship to a higher level from the previously stated good-neighbourly partnership to closer ties between China and Nepal. China's top legislator, Wu Bangguo,[38] during an interaction with Madhav Nepal clarified that the objective of the comprehensive partnership was strategic. This joint statement further widened the window of opportunities for China in Nepal. Madhav Kumar Nepal's successor, Jhalanath Khanal further facilitated Chinese presence in Nepal. A scholar observed that although both Madhav Nepal and Prime Minister Khanal belong to the same party (CPN-UML), the latter, who became prime minister through a secret deal with Maoist Chairman (Prachanda), is perceived more positively by Beijing.[39]

The growing presence of China in Nepal could be a major challenge for it to maintain a balance between the two neighbours. While earlier, India had a major share in the Nepalese economy and investments, the environment has recently become more competitive for India. Both countries exert pressure on Nepal if it enters into any agreement with the other.

There is also domestic pressure to maintain a balance in the relationship. For example, after the conclusion of the Bilateral Investment Promotion and Protection Agreement (BIPPA) agreement between Nepal and India,[40] there was pressure both from China and some top leaders of the UCPN-M on Bhattarai's government to enter into a similar agreement with China.

In an effort to maintain a balance in the hydro-power sector in Nepal, the Interim Constitutions directive on foreign policy was ignored for the first time in the last four years to allot the West Seti project to China.[41] There has been a constant demand from the radical Maoist factions to allocate more hydro power and infrastructure projects to China in order to neutralise India's influence. However, given the controversies related to the West Seti project and a delay in the process, China sensed a conspiracy. These doubts emanated from Nepalese media stories that the Baburam Bhattarai government was supported by India. This perception was strengthened further when Baburam Bhattarai told the media in advance about Chinese Prime Minister Wen Jiabao's visit to Nepal in December 2011.[42]

Moreover, China has never been comfortable with a pro-India regime in Nepal. It has the impression that such a regime might not take strong action against Tibetan refugees in Nepal. Since China had limited options of replacing the Baburam Bhattarai government, it expressed its displeasure by not responding positively to the Nepal Governments request to fix a meeting between Bhattarai and Wen Jiabao on the sidelines of the UN Conference on Sustainable Development at Rio in June 2012.[43] The message was repeated thereafter when China reportedly facilitated Netra Bikram Chand's visits before the split in the UCPN-M in June 2012 and during an unofficial visit of Ai Ping,[44] where surprisingly, Ai Ping did not meet the prime minister. Although China claimed that it was against the split in the party, surprisingly, it did not put serious pressure on the Baidya faction to merge with the parent party during Baidya's China visit in July 2012.

Rather, China acknowledged that the CPN-Maoist party was a nationalist force.[45] Since the Maoists declared equidistance policy had been a non-starter because of both the domestic situation in Nepal and the regional power balance between India and China, the Maoists had moderated their policy by emphasising on economic and development programmes. They proposed a trilateral cooperation between Nepal, India, and China. The proposal came initially as a triangular strategic dialogue from the UCPN-M chairman, Prachanda, on 26 October, after his five-day visit to attend the Shanghai Expo 2010.[46] This proposal was reiterated by Prachanda after signing the MoU with the Asia Pacific Exchange and Cooperation Foundation (APECF) on 7 November 2012 for the Lumbini development project and again during his official visits to Beijing and New Delhi in April 2013. India was lukewarm about the proposal even before Prachanda could formally discuss this with Indian decision makers. Sensing India's negative response, Prachanda modified his proposal during an interaction with Indian intellectuals on 29 April 2013, and said as quoted – "Trilateral cooperation in various mutual projects in Nepal is very much possible. It is our vision for the future. Let me also clarify that by no means do I wish to undermine or replace our centuries-old bilateral relations."[47]

Since Nepal became a Federal Democratic Republic, the Nepal Government's Committee on International Relations and Human Rights in a 40-page report recommended that Nepal's foreign policy be upgraded in the changed context. The report stated that the Bhutanese, Tibetan, and other refugees were a burden on Nepal, and Nepal should send them back with respect, through bilateral and multilateral diplomatic channels. Tibetan refugees should be allowed to stay, on condition that they do not indulge in anti-China activities, which would affect Nepal's commitment to the one-China policy.[48] Nepal should also formulate an appropriate policy to prevent the entry of refugees from Afghanistan, Sudan, and Somalia. The report recommended that the scope of Nepalese foreign policy be diversified to support the economic and social development of the country and that Nepal should also remain committed to international organisations like the UN, World Bank, International Monetary Fund (IMF), Asian Development Bank (ADB), and World Trade Centers (WTC) Association.[49]

Various regimes in Nepal have linked their own insecurity with the country's sovereignty and territorial integrity to ensure their own survival and their leaders have resorted to blaming India to cover up for their own acts of omission and commission.[50] Nepal needs to give priority to its neighbours security concerns. In this connection, pioneer Nepali diplomat Yadunath Khanal's observation is pertinent, "Nepal's foreign policy will break down at the point where either India or China loses faith in Nepal."[51]

Hydro Power

India and Nepal have a power exchange agreement since 1971 for meeting the power requirements in the border areas of the two countries, taking advantage of each other's transmission infrastructure. There are more than twenty 132 kV, 33 kV and 11 kV transmission interconnections which are used both for power exchange in the bordering areas and for power trade.[52]

Nepal has considerable scope for exploiting its potential in hydropower, with an estimated 42,000 MW of commercially feasible capacity. Nepal has signed trade and investment agreements with India, China, and other countries, but political uncertainty and a difficult business climate have hampered foreign investment.[53]

Water resource is considered the backbone of Nepalese economy. With a view to optimizing the benefits and addressing the problems, both Governments have set up three-tier mechanisms called the Joint Ministerial

Commission for Water Resources (JMCWR), Joint Committee on Water Resources (JCWR) and Joint Standing Technical Committee (JSTC) to implement agreements and treaties and also address water-induced problems of flood and inundation.[54] The hydropower potential of Nepal's rivers, based on ex average flow, has been estimated at 83,000 MW. The technical feasibility for development could yield an estimated 44,000 MW. Preliminary studies have identified the potential of over half a dozen medium and large hydroelectric projects which are of greatest value for Nepal from the perspective of exporting hydroelectric power to neighbouring countries.[55]

Two mechanisms, Joint Working Group (JWG) and Joint Steering Committee (JSC) envisaged under the agreement have been established. Joint Technical Team (JTT) was formed for preparation of a long-term integrated transmission plan covering projects up to 2035. The sixth meetings of the JWG and JSC on power cooperation was held in Pokhara, Nepal, on 23 January 2019 and 24 January 2019.[56]

Several hydropower projects are underway in Nepal. Nepal concluded a much-awaited power trade agreement with India in 2014 paving the way for the trade of electric power just like other marketable commodities. This now ensures predictability of the market once electricity is produced.[57] Private/public power developers from India have reached agreements with the Investment Board of Nepal to develop two mega hydropower projects – Upper Karnali and Arun III.[58]

The Transit Treaty was renewed on 5 January 2013 for seven years. The partnership with India in the areas of trade and transit is a matter of utmost importance to Nepal. India is Nepal's largest trading partner. India has provided transit facility to Nepal for third country trade. Both the public and private sectors of India have invested in Nepal. Trade statistics reveal a phenomenal increase in the volume of bilateral trade over the years between the two countries. However, Nepal has an escalating trade deficit with India. Nepal and India have concluded a bilateral Treaty of Transit, Treaty of Trade and the Agreement of Cooperation to Control Unauthorized Trade.[59]

The two countries have concluded a Rail Services Agreement (RSA) and a revised Air Services Agreement (ASA) to enhance bilateral connectivity. India also remains Nepal's largest source of foreign investment and Indian investments in Nepal amount to Rs. 2,175.5 crore with 525 FDI projects. India accounts for 46 per cent of the total foreign investments in Nepal. In October-November 2011, the two countries had also concluded the BIPPA and the Double Taxation Avoidance Agreement (DTAA) which provide a legal framework for enhancing Indian investment into Nepal and further integrating the two economies.[60]

Territorial and Border Issues

The ruggedness of the Nepal-China boundary is clearly revealed by its length which is 1,415 kilometres, while the Nepal-India boundary which runs along three sides of Nepal is 1,580 kilometres, 165 kilometres longer than the Nepal-China boundary. So far as the Nepal-India boundary is concerned, the mountainous portions of the boundary lie in Sikkim State and Darjeeling district of West Bengal State in the east, while the rest of the boundary runs along the plains in the south and along the Mahakali River in the west.

India-Nepal Educational Connect

Over the years, India's contribution to the development of human resources in Nepal has been one of the major aspects of bilateral cooperation. The Government of India provides around 3,000 scholarships/seats annually to Nepali nationals for various courses at the Ph.D./Master's, Bachelor's and plus-two levels in India and in Nepal. These scholarships cover a wide spectrum of disciplines including engineering, medicine, agriculture, pharmacology, veterinary sciences, computer application, business administration, music, and fine arts.[61]

India-Nepal Cultural Connect

Indian initiatives to promote people-to-people contacts in the area of art and culture, academics and media include cultural programmes, symposia and events organized in partnership with different local bodies of Nepal, as well as conferences and seminars in Hindi. Familiarization visits to India by Nepalese journalists/editors and short-term training in India for Nepalese editors/journalists/experts/officials in the field of print and electronic media are also arranged. Assistance is also provided to several India-Nepal friendship organizations working to promote Indian culture and India-Nepal bilateral relations. A MoU between the Sahitya Kala Akademi (India) and the Nepal Academy is already in operation. Four more MoUs have been signed between Doordarshan and Nepal TV, Press Council of India and Press Council of Nepal, Lalit Kala Akademi, India and Nepal Academy of Fine Arts, and a MoU on Youth Exchange between the Governments of India and Nepal. MoUs between India's Sangeet Natak Akademi, and the Nepal Academy of Music & Drama, and between Akashvani, All India Radio (AIR), India and Radio Nepal are under consideration to promote cultural and information exchanges between the two countries.

The Governments of India and Nepal have signed three sister-city agreements for twinning of Kathmandu-Varanasi, Lumbini-Bodhgaya and Janakpur-Ayodhya. India is establishing an e-library system across Nepal. The setting up of a light and sound show at Lumbini with Indian assistance is under process. The Archaeological Survey of India (ASI) is involved in the renovation of the Pashupatinath Temple Complex in Kathmandu. Two ASI teams have already visited Kathmandu to assess the work to be done for conservation/restoration of the Pashupatinath shrine, for which a MoU is under consideration.[62]

An Indian cultural centre was set up in Nepal in August 2007 to showcase the best of Indian culture not only in the capital city but in the areas outside Kathmandu. The Indian Cultural Centre in Kathmandu has generated considerable goodwill through the various cultural events it has undertaken in the past. The Nepal-Bharat Library was founded in 1951 in Kathmandu. It is regarded as the first foreign library in Nepal. Its objective is to enhance and strengthen cultural relations and information exchange between India and Nepal.[63]

The B.P. Koirala India-Nepal Foundation was set up in 1991 through a MoU signed between the governments of India and Nepal. The Foundations objective is to foster educational, cultural, scientific, and technical cooperation between India and Nepal and promote mutual understanding and cooperation through sharing of knowledge and professional talents in academic pursuits and technical specialization.[64]

Socio-Cultural Ties

Social Welfare Initiatives: India had played a leading role in helping the Nepal Army in its modernization through provision of equipment and training. More than 250 training slots are provided every year for training of Nepal Army personnel in various Indian Army training institutions. The Chief of Army Staff of the Indian Army is given the honorary rank of a General in the Nepal Army and a reciprocal honour is conferred on the Chief of the Nepal Army. As of now, we have over 1.26 lakh ex-servicemen residing in Nepal. The Government of India has established the Indian Ex-Servicemen's Welfare Organisation in Nepal (IEWON).[65] The Ex-servicemen's Contributory Health Scheme (ECHS) was launched in Nepal during 2012 vide which free medical treatment to Indian ex-serviceman of Nepal domicile and their dependents is provided within Nepal.[66] This will be discussed further.

Strong Cultural Ties: The Embassy of India, Kathmandu, and the B.P. Koirala India-Nepal Foundation (BPKF) organized several events to promote people-to-people contacts in areas of culture, art, technology, academics and media during the year. The Indo-Nepal Youth Conference in which eminent young professionals from film, fashion, music, literature and business took part was held at the Nepal Tourism Board in Kathmandu on 13-14 May 2012.[67] The Embassy and BPKF in association with the South Asia Foundation, Nepal Tourism Board and the Government of Goa organized the India-Nepal Crafts Exhibition which was inaugurated by the President of Nepal on 27 April 2012 at the Nepal Academy in Kathmandu. The President also inaugurated the function to celebrate the 150th birth anniversary of Mahamana Madan Mohan Malaviya on 30 November and 1 December 2012.[68]

To address Indian concerns over the use of Nepalese territory for terror activities directed at India, the authorities were directed to ensure that the unique open borders were not misused by devious elements posing security threats to either side. An agreement was also reached on finalizing the texts of an extradition and mutual legal assistance treaties at an early date. Officials were directed to expedite the signing of a memorandum of understanding on a police academy. The need to explore ways to enhance sub-regional cooperation, particularly in the areas of trade, transit, connectivity and hydropower were also discussed.[69]

As regards pending India-Nepal boundary issues, formation of the Boundary Working Group (BWG) to undertake construction was welcomed, with the task of restoration and repair of boundary pillars, including clearance of no-man's land and other technical tasks. Officials were also asked to expedite construction of cross-border railway at all five agreed border points and the four integrated check posts (ICPs) to facilitate trade and transit as well as Nepal's export to and import from third countries. On Nepal's request, the Indian side agreed to take up the project for the construction of the Raxaul-Amlekhgunj petroleum pipeline in the first phase and extend it to Kathmandu in the next phase to facilitate the transport of petroleum products.[70]

Referring to the socio-cultural ties, the Prime Minister emphasized on the close Army-to-Army bonds and the continued sacrifice of Nepali origin Gorkha soldiers, and underlined this exemplary commitment the people of Nepal had displayed in securing India. Much to the relief of the people of Nepal, the confirmation of Lumbini as the birthplace of Lord Buddha was clearly highlighted.

In Kathmandu, a popular narrative that had taken hold regarding an absence of Indian political engagement, and assertion by bureaucrats and security and intelligence agencies was corrected by Modi and shown to Nepal how important the country was to the highest Indian executive.[71]

21st Century: Continuing Political Instability

The political instability within Nepal undermines the special relationship the two countries share and this difficult phase will continue unless both countries re-assess their approach towards each other, identifying areas and mechanisms of cooperation which not only have the approval and consensus of all interested parties but also enhance the unique relations the two countries share in abundance.

At a time when India is confronted with growing negative sentiments in Nepal, China has been reaping a good harvest of positive perceptions. Despite the delay in signing the oil trade agreement and slow progress in reopening the existing Nepal-China trading routes, there has been a phenomenal improvement of Chinese influence and popularity in Nepal over the last few months.

Madhesi Agitation

A strong political movement seeking enlarged participation of the Terai in Nepal's politics and policymaking emerged in 2007, decisively setting the agenda for federalism.

India-Nepal relations had reached their lowest ebb. India foresaw that the Madhesi agitation could have a spillover effect. On the other hand, there was a strong perception in Nepal that the Madhesi movement intensified especially due to the tacit support it received from India.[72] The conflict between the plains and Kathmandu manifested itself post the promulgation of Nepal's new Constitution – in the two-week Madhesi blockade of goods, which appeared to have India's unofficial backing.[73]

The slow movement of cargo from India and the shortage of essential commodities in Nepal due to the agitation in the Madhesh region have been perceived as an unofficial India imposed blockade on Nepal. Some radical Maoist groups have taken advantage of the situation and attacked the Arun III project office, which is being constructed by the Satluj Jal Vidyut Nigam (SJVN). Media reports also indicated that suspected Maoists attacked the GMR Energy office in Kathmandu and GMR's Upper Karnali hydropower project in Surkhet district. Earlier, the Cable Operators Association of Nepal stopped broadcasting Indian television channels.[74]

The political crisis in Nepal had led to either cancellation or postponement of regular bilateral meetings between India and Nepal on a host of issues. No substantial progress has been made with regard to the 10 MoUs signed during Prime Minister Narendra Modi's visit to Kathmandu in November 2014. There are reports of an increase in the activities of Pakistan-based terrorists and the circulation of fake Indian currency.[75] If Nepal gets an oil pipeline from China, the contours of politics in the Himalayan border region of India could change.[76]

The gains for China will always be disproportionately higher than the losses that India would incur if there is a prolonged crisis in the Madhesh region. At the same time, leaving the Madhesis high and dry in the present situation, when there is a perception in Madhesh that India might reverse its course to placate the leadership in the hill region, could complicate the Nepalese situation. There is a need, therefore, to engage leaders of all political parties and craft another consensus. This can ensure Nepalese unity and integrity at one level and cement India-Nepal ties on the other.[77]

NOTES

1. Muni, S D. *India and Nepal: A Changing Relationship*, Konark Publishers, 1992, p. 237.
2. Ibid.
3, Karki, R. Lessons Unlearnt, *Republica,* 3 February 2016 at http://e.myrepublica.com/2015 /index.php?option=com_k2&view=item&id=36372:lessons-unlearnt&Itemid=267 accessed on 5 March 2016.
4. Baral. LR. Nepals Security Policy and South Asian Regionalism, *Asian Survey*, vol. 26, issue: 11, November 1986, pp. 1207-1219.
5. Thapliyal, S. *Mutual Security: The case of India-Nepal.* Lancer Publishers: New Delhi, 1992, p. 104.
6. Muni, S D. *India and Nepal: A Changing Relationship*. Konark Publishers, 1992, pp. 23-25.
7. Ibid.
8. Sharma, G. Anti-India Protests erupt in Nepal over shooting death on border, *Reuters*, athttp:// www.reuters.com/article/us-nepal-india/anti-india-protests-erupt-in-nepal-over-shooting-death-on-border-idUSKBN16H1CS accessed on 2 August 2017.
9. Muni, S.D. op. cit., p. 98.
10. Rai, B. Gorkhas The Warrior Race, 2009, p. 51.
11. Rose, L.E. *Nepal Strategy for Survival*, Oxford University Press, Bombay, 1971, p. 248.
12. Yogi, N.N & Acharya, B (eds.). *Rashtrapita Shri 5 Bada Maharaj Prithvi Narayan Shah Divyopadesh*, Divine Counsel of Shri 5 Maharaj Prithvi Narayan Shah the Great, Kathmandu,1951, pp. 18-19.
13. Central Intelligence Agency (CIA). *The World Fact Book*, cia.gov/library/publications/the-world-factbook/geos/np.html
14. Shah, S.K. *India's Foreign Policy: Past, Present and Ties with the World*, Vij Books India Pvt. Ltd., 2017, pp. 55-58.
15. Farzand, A. Nepal: Wake-Up Call, Interview: CP Bastol, *India Today*, 19 June 2000, at http://www.india.today.com/itoday/20000619/neighbours.html accessed on 10 August 2017.
16. Ministry of External Affairs, Government of India. Fact sheet-India and Nepal Partnership, at http://www.mea.gov.in /press-releases.htm? dtl /21920/Fact +Sheet+India Nepal + Partnership accessed on 9 July 2013.
17. Ministry of Foreign Affairs, Government of Nepal. Nepal-India relations, https://mofa.gov.np/nepal-india-relations/#:~:text=Nepal%2DIndia%20relations%20are%2C%20in,ties%20between%20the%20two%20countries
18. Central Intelligence Agency. https://www.cia.gov/library/publications/the-world-factbook/geos/np.html

19. Upreti, Bishnu Raj (2006). *Armed Conflict and Peace Process in Nepal*, Adroit Publishers.
20. Upreti, 2006:24.
21. Ibid.
22. Ibid.
23. Bhattarai, R. (2004). *Geopolitical Specialties of Nepal and a Regional Approach to Conflict Transformation*, Kathmandu: Friends for Peace.
24. Kumar, D. and Sharma, H. (2004). *Security Sector Reform in Nepal: Challenges and Opportunities*, Kathmandu: Friends for Peace.
25. Upreti. 2006:24.
26. Ibid., 38.
27. 40 Point Demand, 4 February 1996, https://www.satp.org/satporgtp/countries/nepal/document/papers/40points.htm
28. Ibid.
29. Gajurel, C.P. No Special relation between Nepal and India, *The Telegraph Weekly*, 25 December 2008, at http://www.telegraphnepal.com/backup/telegraph/ news_det.php?news _id+4576 accessed on 16 July 2013. The paper was formally submitted at the Institute of Foreign Affairs-FES (Friedrich Ebert Stiftung, Germany) Seminar in Kathmandu, 23 December 2008. C.P. Gajurel wrote this while he was a Politburo member of the Communist Party of Nepal (Maoist). He is presently vice-chairman of the Communist Party of Nepal-Maoist (Mohan Baidya faction). This faction in January 2013 identified India as its Principal Enemy.
30. Promoting Transboundary Tourism in Mapchya Rural Municipality, Humla, Kailash Sacred Landscape, Nepal, International Centre for Integrated Mountain Development (ICIMOD) Proceedings, 2017, p.1.
31. Basnet, P. China's Success, *Himal Southasian*, April 2011 athttp://himalmag.com/component/content/article/4350-chinas-success-html accessed on 13 July 2013.
32. Marasini, P. First political visit will be to India: Prachanda, *The Hindu*, 28 August 2008, at http://www.thehindu.com/todays-paper/tp-international/First-political-visit-will-be-to-India-Prachanda/article15290816.ece accessed on 12 March 2016.
33. Lee, P. Sino-Indian rivalry fuels Nepals turmoil, *Asia Times*, 14 November 2009, at http://www.atimes.com/atimes/South_Asia/KK14Df01.html accessed on 13 July 2013. For more information see Anand Gurung, Reversal of Role: Is China playing Nepal Card now? Canada Tibet Committee, 6 March 2006, at http://www.tibet.ca/en/newsroom/wtn/5641 accessed on 13 July 2013. Also see China agrees to provide Rs 200 million worth security assistance, *Nepal News*, Kathmandu, 7 December 2008.
34. Nepal PM Prachanda can revert to tradition, likely to visit India ahead of China, *The Times of India*, 18 August 2016, at https://timesofindia.indiatimes.com/world/Nepal-PM-Prachanda-can-revert-to-tradition-likely-to-visit-India-ahead-of-China/articleshow/53756902.cms accessed on 30 March 2017.
35. PM in Norway, holds talks on energy deal, *The Rising Nepal*, 29 March 2009 at http://democracyandclasstruggle.blogspot.in/2009/03/prime-minister-prachanda-innorway.html accessed on 13 July 2013.
36. Pradhan, S. Madhav Kumar asks Maoists to join New Govt., *Outlook*, 26 May 2009, at https://www.outlookindia.com/newswire/story/madhav-kumar-asks-maoists-to-join-new-govt/660441/?next accessed on 30 March 2017.
37. Ministry of External Affairs, Government of India. Joint Press Statement on the Official Visit of the Prime Minister of Nepal, New Delhi, https://www.mea.gov.in/press-

releases.htm?dtl/5214/Joint+Press+Statement+ on+the+Official+ Visit+of+the+Prime+ Minister+ of+ Nepal

38. China, Nepal to advance bilateral ties (2009, December 30). *Xinhua* (English), 30 December 2009, at http:/news.xinhuanet.com/English/2009-12/30/content_12731012. htm accessed on 13 July 2013.
39. Joint statement on China, Nepal to advance bilateral ties, at http:// www.fmprc.gov.cn/ eng/wjdt/2649/t649608.htm accessed on 12 February 2014.
40. Agreement between The Government of Nepal and The Government of India for The Promotion and Protection of Investments, at https://www.indianembassy.org.np/doing-business/BIPPA-india-Nepal-21-oct-2011-ENG.pdf accessed 30 July 2013.
41. Sharma, R.D. NEA, CTGI seal deal on 75mw West Seti Hydropower Project.
42. Krishnan, A. Wen Jiabao makes brief Nepal visit, offers aid,, *The Hindu*, 14 January 2012 at http://www.thehindu.com/news/international/Wen-Jiabao-makes-brief-Nepal-visit-offers-aid/article13366452.ece accessed on 12 March 2016.
43. *Current Affairs.* June 2012 Magazine, at https://www.scribd.com/document/99483482/ Current-Affairs-June-2012-Magazine accessed on 12 March 2016.
44. Vice-Minister of International Department for South Asian Affairs of the Communist Party of China (CPC).
45. Chinese leaders caution Baidya against foreign interests in federalism, *Nepal News*, 26 July 2012 at http://www.nepalnews.com/archive/2012/jul/jul26/news18.php accessed on 31 July 2012.
46. Dahal returns from China; prescribes trilateral talks for strategy on Nepal, *Nepal News*, 27 October 2010 at http://www.nepalnews.com/home/index.php/news/2/10090-dahalreturns-from China accessed on 31 July 2012.
47. Vision for tomorrow: India –Nepal Ties, *República*, 29 April 2013 at http:// www.myrepublica.com/portal/index.php?action=news_details&news_id=53965 accessed on 12 July 2013.
48. Government of Nepal, Ministry of Foreign Affairs. Nepal-China Relations, Kathmandu at http://mofa.gov.np/nepal-china-relations/ accessed on 30 August 2016.
49. Behera Anshuman. Nepal. The Constituent Assembly That Was, Published by IDSA (2012), pp. 1-3.
50. Ghimire, Y. Next door Nepal: Blaming it on India, *The Indian Express*, 5 October 2015, at http://indianexpress.com/article/opinion/ columns/next-door-Nepal-blaming-it-on-India/ accessed on 12 March 2016.
51. Cited in Acharya, M.D. A dignified and principled foreign policy is what Nepal needs, Telegraph Nepal, at http://www.telegraphnepal.com/national/2014-12-11/a-dignified-and-principled-foreign-policy-is-what-nepal-needs.html accessed on 12 March 2015.
52. Ministry of External Affairs, Government of India. India-Nepal relations, mea.gov.in/ Portal/ForeignRelation/India-Nepal_Bilateral_Brief_September_2019.pdf
53. Central Intelligence Agency. https://www.cia.gov/library/publications/the-world-factbook/geos/np.html
54. Status and Implementation of Transboundary River Agreements on the Kosi River in Nepal, Issue Brief No. 1, April 2015, pp. 3-4.
55. Nepal-India Cooperation on Hydropower (NICOH) (2006). Executive summary published by Independent Power Producers Association, Nepal Confederation of Indian Industry (2006), p. 7.
56. Ministry of External Affairs, Government of India. India-Nepal relations, mea.gov.in/ Portal/ForeignRelation/India-Nepal_Bilateral_Brief_September_2019.pdf

57. Ministry of Foreign Affairs. *Investment In Nepal*, https://mofa.gov.np/about-nepal/investment-in-nepal/
58. Ministry of Foreign Affairs, Government of Nepal. *Nepal-India Relations*, https://mofa.gov.np/nepal-india-relations/
59. Ministry of Foreign Affairs, Government of Nepal. Nepal-India Relationship, ttps://mofa.gov.np/nepal-india-relations/
60. Ibid.
61. Ibid.
62. Ibid.
63. Ibid.
64. Ibid.
65. Ibid.
66. Analysis of Nepalese PMs visit to India, Institute of Defence Studies and Analyses, at https://idsa.in/accessed on 4 November 2011.
67. Embassy of Nepal, New Delhi. Socio Cultural Relations.
68. India-Nepal Relations,, at http://mea.gov.in/Portal/ForeignRelation/India_Nepal_Relations_ 11_04_2017.pdf accessed on 30 August 2017.
69. Sarkar, D. India must check who comes in through its open international borders, *The Economic Times*, 27 February 2017, at https://economictimes.indiatimes.com/news/defence/india-must-check-who-comes-in-through-its-open-international-borders/articleshow/57377564.cms accessed on 30 August 2017.
70. Nepal-India BWG meeting signs Agreed Minutes between two sides, *The Kathmandu Post*, 30 August 2017, at http://kathmandupost.ekantipur.com/news/2017-08-30/nepal-india-boundary-working-group-meeting.html accessed on 30 August 2017.
71. Ghimire, Y. Next door Nepal: Blaming it on India, *The Indian Express*, 5 October 2015, at http://indianexpress.com/article/opinion/columns/next-door-nepal-blaming-it-on-india/ accessed on 12 March 2016.
72. Nayak, N. R. Nepals pronounced pro-China tilt, *The Hindu: Business Line*, 17 January 2016 at http://www.thehindubusinessline.com/opinion/nepals-pronounced-prochina-tilt/article8116824.ece accessed on 30 August 2017.
73. Ghimire, Yubaraj. Who are the Madhesis, why are they angry, *The Indian Express*, 5 October 2015, https://indianexpress.com/article/explained/who-are-the-madhesis-why-are-they-angry/
74. Ibid.
75. Ibid.
76. Ibid.
77. Ibid.

2

Important Bilateral Security Fault Lines and Their Effects

Review of the Existing Peace and Friendship Treaty, 1950

The Treaty of Peace and Friendship was concluded between India and Nepal in July 1950.[1] A copy of the extracts of the treaty is placed at Appendix A. The Letters Exchanged is an adjunct to the treaty and these extracts are placed at Annexure to Appendix A. The treaty consists of 10 Articles. Article I acknowledge complete sovereignty, territorial integrity and independence of both countries. Vide Article II, both governments agreed to inform each other of any serious friction or misunderstanding with neighbouring states likely to cause breach of friendly relations between the two governments. Articles II, V and Letters Exchanged bind the security interests of both countries. Article V allowed Nepal to import warlike stores from India and others but NOT through Indian territory without India's permission. India did not anticipate arms supply by or through China.[2] The Letters Exchanged explicitly states that neither government shall tolerate any threat to the security of the other by a foreign aggressor, for which they should consult each other. The aggressor, in the case of Nepal, could only be China.

From the Letters Exchanged along with the Treaty of Peace and Friendship, 1950, it was clear that Nepal had joined India in a unified system of defence and had agreed to subject certain aspects of its external affairs and external trade to India's guidance. This era of special relations continued till 1955, when King Mahendra ascended to the throne, though, even during this period, many dissensions arose.[3] It was felt that the Ranas (hereditary Prime Ministers) in power had sold out national integrity and that the treaty allowed too much Indian political interference.

Nepal's cordial relations with China and Pakistan, membership of the UN and need to remain equidistant from India and China prompted greater demands for a review of the 1950 treaty. Pressures from China could also be responsible for this. In 1967, consequent to the Chinese cultural revolution, China demanded that facilities similar to those given to India be granted to them, as well, that is, recruitment of Gorkhas in the People's Liberation Army (PLA), the right to post their personnel on the India-Nepal border, and free trade and transit facilities for the Chinese.

Articles VI and VII provide for socio-economic cooperation. Article VI states that nationals of either country be allowed similar treatment in economic development.[4] It also acknowledged the need to provide protection to Nepalese in Nepal from unrestricted competition from Indian businesses for a few years, though no formal agreement has been concluded in this respect.[5] Article VII provided reciprocally mutual privileges in matters of transit, residence, and the like, in each other's countries. Both these have benefitted Nepal immensely. However, King Mahendra imposed restrictions on purchase of property in Nepal by Indians citing the reason that Nepal was not in a position to allow free immigration because of its size, population, and economy.[6] In doing so, they claim that similar restrictions exist within India as well, in the case of Jammu and Kashmir and the north-eastern states.

Any new treaty/treaties if and when negotiated would need to make the following adjustments for interests of both countries:

(a) Article II which targets Sino-Nepalese relations needs to be reworded with a wider world view. It may be more appropriate to consult each other on international perspectives and regional affairs from time to time other than restrict consultations to the neighbour (China) factor only.

(b) The Letters Exchanged which restrict Nepal's import of war-like stores through India without agreement of the Government of India, needs reconsideration.

(c) Articles VI and VII along with Para 1 of the Letters Exchanged along with the treaty enshrines the entire gamut of special relations between the two countries. One cannot exist without the other. Nepal needs to recognize this and it cannot expect all advantages without catering to basic Indian national interests.

The Treaty, however, has for various reasons become an emotional issue in Nepal and the demand for its abrogation has regularly featured in the election manifestos of different political parties. The Rana regime fell within six months of signing it. Subsequent regimes in Nepal have continually expressed their reservations over the Treaty. However, the people of Terai who have strong links with people across the border in India want the continuation of this Treaty. One of the significant parts of this Treaty has been the granting of resident status to each other's citizens. Although Nepal does not reciprocate this clause, it has enabled many Nepalese citizens to take up government jobs in India. Over time, Nepal has enacted much legislation to dilute the original spirit of this Treaty. The monarchy too believed this Treaty was an instrument of Indian influence.

The Treaty has been politicised over time to serve the political interests of the particular constituency that it draws its support from anti-India sentiments in Nepal. With the introduction of multi-party democracy in Nepal in 1990, other issues such as border encroachment, hydro projects, etc., were taken up by some political parties. In 1994, for example, the CPN-UML campaigned vigorously on these issues. The 40 demands of the CPN (Maoist) in 1995 also focused on the 1950 Treaty and aroused intense anti-India feelings especially within the Kathmandu Valley, during the People's War. However, except for King Mahendra, no other monarch raised this issue with India.[7]

During the constitutional monarchy period, the Nepalese Foreign Minister Kamal Thapa of the royalist Rashtriya Prajatantra Party (RPP), a coalition partner of the Nepali Congress which led the government visited India in August 1998 with a non-paper, which, for the first time, made some suggestions for its revision. The CPN (Maoist), in its manifesto for the 2008 Constituent Assembly (CA) elections, promised to abrogate the Treaty and maintain equal distance between India and China. The CPN-UML also promised to review all unequal treaties, while the NC manifesto remained silent on the matter. Yet, even after India expressed its willingness to revise the Treaty, there has been a lack of political consensus in Nepal over the issue and no alternative or specific proposal has been given by Nepal regarding the provisions they want to revise.[8]

The politicisation of this Treaty is also evident from the fact that no political party wants to abrogate it. In September 2008, India and Nepal agreed to form a high-level committee headed by their foreign secretaries to examine the Treaty and suggest possible revisions. There is a view in India, however, that this issue is being needlessly hyped. For instance, former Indian ambassador to Nepal, Deb Mukherjee, in an interview to *The Telegraph* in May 2008 said:

> This demand has been raised several times in the past and we [India] have said, fair enough, renegotiate or restructure. In fact, Clause 10 of the treaty clearly says it can be abrogated by either side on a year's notice. And I remember that during the Foreign Secretary-level talks in 2001, we had reminded the Nepali delegation of the clause and said, why don't you do it? We should be prepared to discuss all options.[9]

India's former Foreign Secretary Shyam Saran also dismissed the contention of Prachanda that the Treaty was an unequal pact, and pointed out that under the pact Nepali citizens enjoy special privileges in India. The issue figured prominently in the joint statement during the visit of Prachanda to New Delhi.[10]

The two countries agreed to review, adjust and update the Treaty and other agreements, while duly considering the special features of the bilateral relationship. From an Indian perspective, the Treaty seems to have limited relevance in the changed global security environment. India's former Indian Ambassador to Nepal, K.V. Rajan, observed:

> Its relevance for India's security in today's context is limited and questionable. China is no longer the only security concern in the sub region. Pakistani activities in and through Nepal ... environment and climate change, also have serious long-term implications for the security of both countries.[11]

Apart from addressing mutual security concerns, the Treaty also covers other social-economic issues. It has been observed that people have criticised more the letter of exchange that followed the Treaty than the Treaty itself. Nevertheless, both countries have periodically acknowledged each other's value and importance and have also described the relationship as special on various occasions. For example, Maoist leader and former Prime Minister Baburam Bhattarai noted: Practically, we are more closely integrated with India, with an open border and closer economic ties. So, we have more interaction with India and more problems also, which sometimes creates misunderstanding.[12] Therefore, in view of the changed geopolitical dynamics, the Treaty should be updated in accordance with contemporary reality.

There appears to be a growing realisation in Nepal of the many advantages that accrue to them because of the special provisions that exist in the Treaty. Recent events also give some indication that the Government of Nepal may itself not be inclined to scrap it. India cannot afford deepening anti-India sentiments in Nepal as that would be very detrimental in the long run, nor can it allow itself into providing concessions without necessary responses.[13]

Boundary Related Disputes

Indo-Nepalese boundary disputes are both the legacy of British colonisation as well as the vagaries of nature. Boundary disputes along its southern and south-eastern borders are mainly due to shifting river beds as a result of heavy drainage as shown in the figure 2.1 which illustrates the shifting courses of the river Kosi.

In a number of places, where boundary pillars mark the boundary between the two countries, these have been washed away. There have been encroachments from both sides, on each other's territory. The longer the

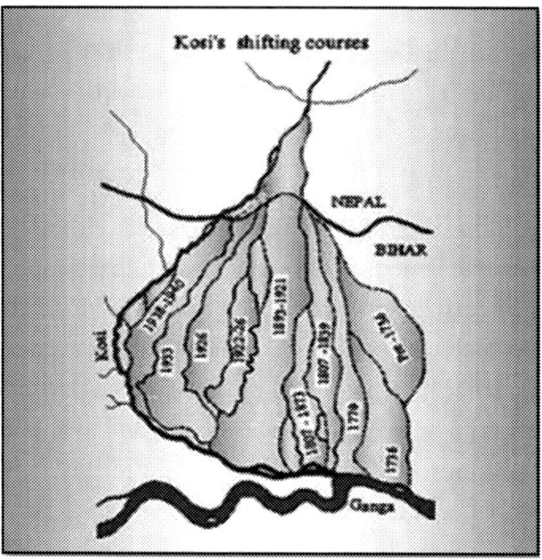

Map 2.1: Map showing Shifting Courses of the Kosi River[14]

dispute remains, the more difficult it will be to resolve. Boundary problem-solving is further complicated by the involvement of the centre, the states concerned and internal politics of the region which caters more to the vote bank than long-term national issues. Specific issues relating to the dispute are given in the following paragraphs.

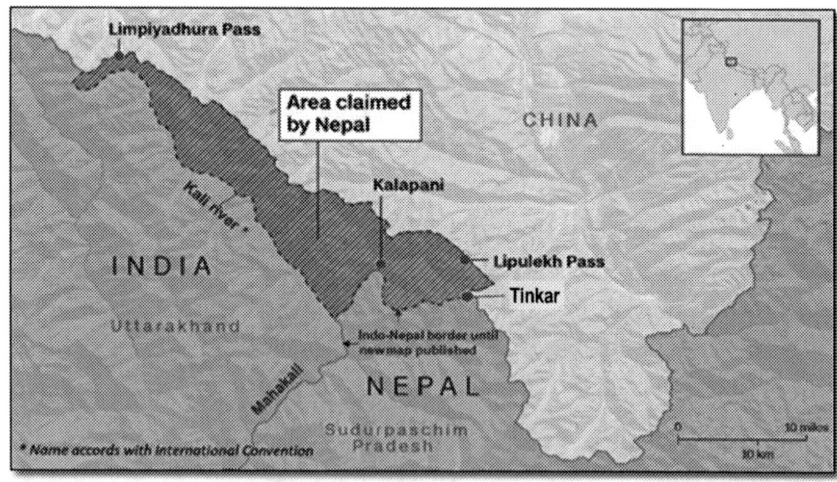

Map 2.2: India-Nepal Disputed Area

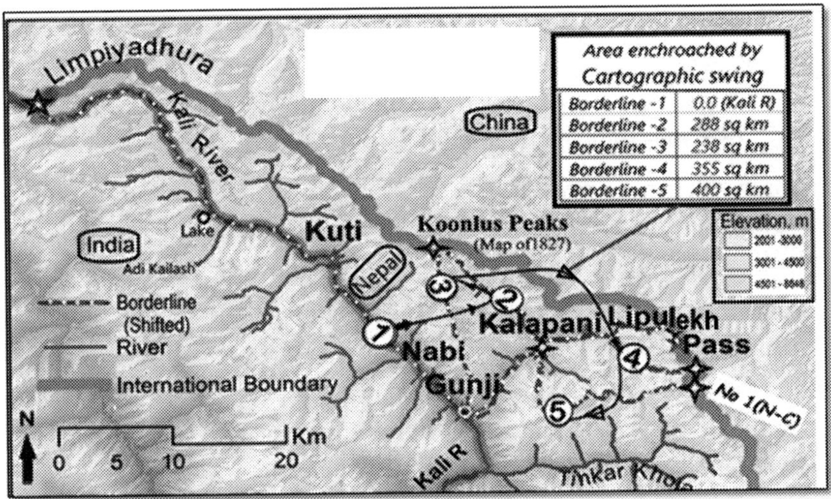

Map 2.3: India-Nepal Disputed Area

Explaining the Kalapani Border Issue

Historically, Kalapani is a 35-square kilometre area claimed by India and Nepal after the ratification of the Mahakali treaty with India by Nepal's Parliament, it has been embroiled in controversy since mid-1996.

The Kalapani river is the eastern headwaters of the Kali river, near the borders of Nepal and Kumaon (Uttarakhand) in India.[15] It shares a border on the north with the Tibet Autonomous Region of China and Nepal in the east and south. The area is in India's control but Nepal claims the region because of historical and cartographic reasons. It originates from small springs and runs through an area that includes a disputed area of about 400 square kilometres[16] around the source of the river although the exact size of the disputed area varies from source to source.[17] The river borders the Nepalese zone of Mahakali and the Indian state of Uttarakhand. Subsequent maps drawn by British surveyors show the source of the boundary river at different places. This discrepancy in locating the source of the river led to boundary disputes between India and Nepal, with each country producing maps supporting their claims.

The Kalapani Border Contestation: Views from India and Nepal

India and Nepal have varied interpretations of the river Kali (known as

Kalapani) and its various tributaries that pass through the mountains. The area is the largest territorial dispute between Nepal and India consisting of at least 37,000 hectares of land in the High Himalayas. The Kalapani region derives its name from the river Kali.

By the Treaty of Sugauli in 1816, India inherited the boundary with Nepal, established between Nepal and the East India Company. The early British survey maps identified the north-west stream, Kuti Yangti, from Limpiyadhura, is the origin, but after 1857 changed the alignment to Lipu Gad, and in 1879 to Pankha Gad, the north-east stream, thus defining the origin as just below Kalapani. Nepal accepted the change and India inherited this boundary in 1947. Official sources in India claim that the administrative and revenue records dating back to 1830s (available with the UP-state government), show that Kalapani area has traditionally been administered as part of Pithoragarh district.[18]

According to India, vide Article 5 of the Sugauli Treaty (1816), Nepal had renounced all claims to areas lying west of the river Kali. The Kali (now Mahakali) river thus evolved into a well-identified border demarcation in the west. Before claiming some area around the Kalapani tri-junction, Nepal had disputed even the source of the river Kali, as claimed by India.

Journalist Kallol Bhattacherjee observes that according to the Sugauli treaty:

(a) Nepal lost the regions of Kumaon-Garhwal in the west and Sikkim in the east. According to Article 5, the King of Nepal gave up his claims over the region west of the river Kali which originates in the High Himalayas and flows into the great plains of the Indian subcontinent.

(b) The British rulers recognised Nepal's right to the region that fell to the east of the river Kali. Here lies the historic origin of the dispute.[19]

Nepal has laid claim to all areas east of the Lipu Gad, the rivulet that joins the river Kali on its border, a tri-junction with India and China. The tributaries of the Kali River comprise a number of streams, including the Lipu Gad, which merge into the main river at the Kalapani temple near the tri-junction. The Nepalese contention is that the Lipu Gad is, in fact, the Kali River up to its source to the east of the Lipulekh Pass.[20] India denied the Nepalese contention that Lipu Gad was the Kali River. In the Indian view, the Kali River begins only after Lipu Gad and is joined by other streams arising from the Kalapani springs. Therefore, the Indian border leaves the midstream of river near Kalapani and follows the high watershed of the streams that join it.[21]

Nepal claims that a land mass, high in the mountains that falls to the east of the entire stretch starting from Limpiyadhura downwards, is theirs. India on the other hand says the border begins at Kalapani which India says is where the river begins. Nepali border experts claim that according to the maps published by the then British Surveyor-General of India in the years of 1827 as well as 1856, Kalapani area is clearly depicted as Nepalese territory.

According to Nepal, after the India-China war in 1962, Nepal allowed Indian troops to occupy some posts in Nepal as a defensive measure. India has withdrawn from all of them, except Kalapani. It apparently wants to hold on to that post.

Kumar observes: Nepal has long complained about minor Indian encroachments into other parts of the border, mainly when rivers shift their course from time to time. But Kalapani is different, with India in possession, and this has raised nationalist hackles in Nepal. Nepal claims that the Kalapani area lies within its Darchula district and, therefore, the Indo-Tibetan Border Police (ITBP) presence there amounts to Indian encroachment of Nepal's territory. It has therefore demanded that the border post be removed and the area restored to it.[22]

The bone of contention is the Kalapani-Limpiyadhura-Lipulekh tri-junction between Nepal-India and China (Tibet). Located on the banks of the river Kali at an altitude of 3,600 metres, the Kalapani territory lies at the eastern border of Uttarakhand in India and Nepal's Sudurpaschim Pradesh in the west. Observer Research Foundation's (ORF) Sohini Nayak observes in her ORF Series, that Buddhi Narayan Shrestha, former Director-General of Nepal's Land Survey department, had categorised the debaters into two broad groups:

(a) Views of Elite Community of Nepal: They view that the river which flows to the west of Kalapani is the main River Kali, originating at either Limpiyadhura or the nearby Lipulekh Pass, which are both within the Nepalese territory, thus justifying the area as an inherent part of Nepal.

(b) Views of Nepal-India Technical Level Joint Boundary Working Group, and officials of the Embassy of India in Nepal: River Kali originated from a smaller rivulet named Pankhagad, lying on the southern portion of Kalapani and the subsequent ridge on the eastern part of this area is the true border, and therefore making the territory part of India.[23]

Map 2.4: Limpiyadhura-Kalapani-Lipulekh

Source: Buddhi Narayan Shrestha, Authenticity of Lipulekh Border Pass, June 2015.

The dispute is mainly because of the varying interpretations of the origin of the river and its various tributaries that slice through the mountains. While Nepal's claim of the territory east of Kali is based on the Limpiyadhura origin, India says the river actually takes the name Kali near Kalapani.

According to them, until 1857, all maps produced by British cartographers suggest that the origin of the Kali River lies in the Limpiyadhura Pass. But in the period between 1857 and 1881, a subtle but deliberate attempt to misname the river Kali got under way, write Nepalese geographers Mangal Siddhi Manandhar and Hriday Lal Koirala. Both geographers maintain that the cartographic move on the part of the British was unauthorised, unilateral, and without any agreement with the government of Nepal.[24] The effort to resolve this border Lipulekh-Kalapani has remained unresolved since 1962 as the Indo-Tibetan Border Police are posted there since the India-China war of the same year.

The interaction between the two Heads of State in 2000 during Nepalese Prime Minister Girija Prasad Koirala's visit to New Delhi is significant. The then Indian Prime Minister, Atal Bihari Vajpayee, had agreed to resolve the border dispute through an on-site study of Kalapani, with the aim of concluding it in 2002. Both countries agreed for delineating the Bilateral Joint Boundary Committee. However, there was no progress as India refused to withdraw its troops from the area.[25]

During Nepalese Prime Minister Sushil Koirala's visit to New Delhi to have a discussion with Smt. Sushma Swaraj, both the countries agreed on the bilateral joint boundary committee. However, there was no progress as India refused to withdraw its troops from the area. Both countries agreed to resolve pending Nepal-India boundary issues once and for all ... including Kalapani. At that time, the Nepal-India Joint Ministerial Mechanism decided to resolve the dispute over Kalapani and Susta at the Foreign Secretary level on the basis of technical suggestions.

On the brighter side, the Nepal-India Joint Border Inspection Mechanism of 1981 and the Nepal-India Joint Border Management Committee, formed in 1997, are both noteworthy in the discussion about efforts that were made by both countries in the past.

Organisations like the Nepal-India Joint Technical Level Boundary Committee (JTBC) constituted in 1981 (dissolved in 2008) have mainly worked to bring about a comprehensive border management system along with the re-establishment of the boundary pillars from the British era and the periodic inspection of keeping the boundary intact.[26] These organisations mainly worked to bring about a comprehensive border management system along with the re-establishment of the boundary pillars from the British era and the periodic inspection of keeping the boundary intact. Despite all these efforts, border disputes still persist.[27]

Since the abrogation of Article 370 and 35-A of the Indian Constitution, the former State of Jammu and Kashmir has been bifurcated into two Union Territories (UT) of Jammu and Kashmir, and Ladakh. Immediately after the bifurcation of the state in August 2019, the Survey of India issued a new political map (eighth edition) on 2 November 2019 to reflect the change in the status of Jammu and Kashmir as two Union Territories. However, on 8 November the ninth edition was issued.[28] It was identical to the previous edition but the name of the Kali River had been deleted. Predictably, this led to stronger protests, with Nepal invoking Foreign Secretary-level talks to resolve issues.

Nepal objected to the claims made by India and contended that the region was an unsettled territory of the Darchula district in the country's Sudurpaschim province and issued a statement to resolve through diplomatic channels after assessing the five historical documents, facts, and evidence.[29] A new map of Nepal based on the older British survey reflecting Kali River originating from Limpiyadhura in the north-west of Garbyang was adopted by parliament and notified on 20 May 2020, six months after India made changes to the political map claiming parts of Kalapani as Indian territory. On 22 May a constitutional amendment proposal was tabled to include it in a relevant Schedule.

The new alignment adds 335 square kilometres. to Nepali territory, territory that had never been reflected in a Nepali map for nearly 170 years. The new map claimed Nepal has also claimed a large tract of land across Uttar Pradesh's Gorakhpur in Susta as a part of its territory in the new maps released on 20 May and has since asked India to remove encroachments from the area.[30]

This dispute began after New Delhi issued an official map last year, including the Kalapani and Lipulekh area that Nepal regards as its own. The tension escalated further after India inaugurated the 80-km road in Uttarakhand, which connects close to the Line of Actual Control and opens a new route for the Kailash Mansarovar yatra via the Lipulekh Pass.

Geographers Manandhar and Koirala in their work, *Nepal-India boundary issue: River Kali as international boundary*, claim that since no map attached with the Sugauli Treaty and countersigned by both the

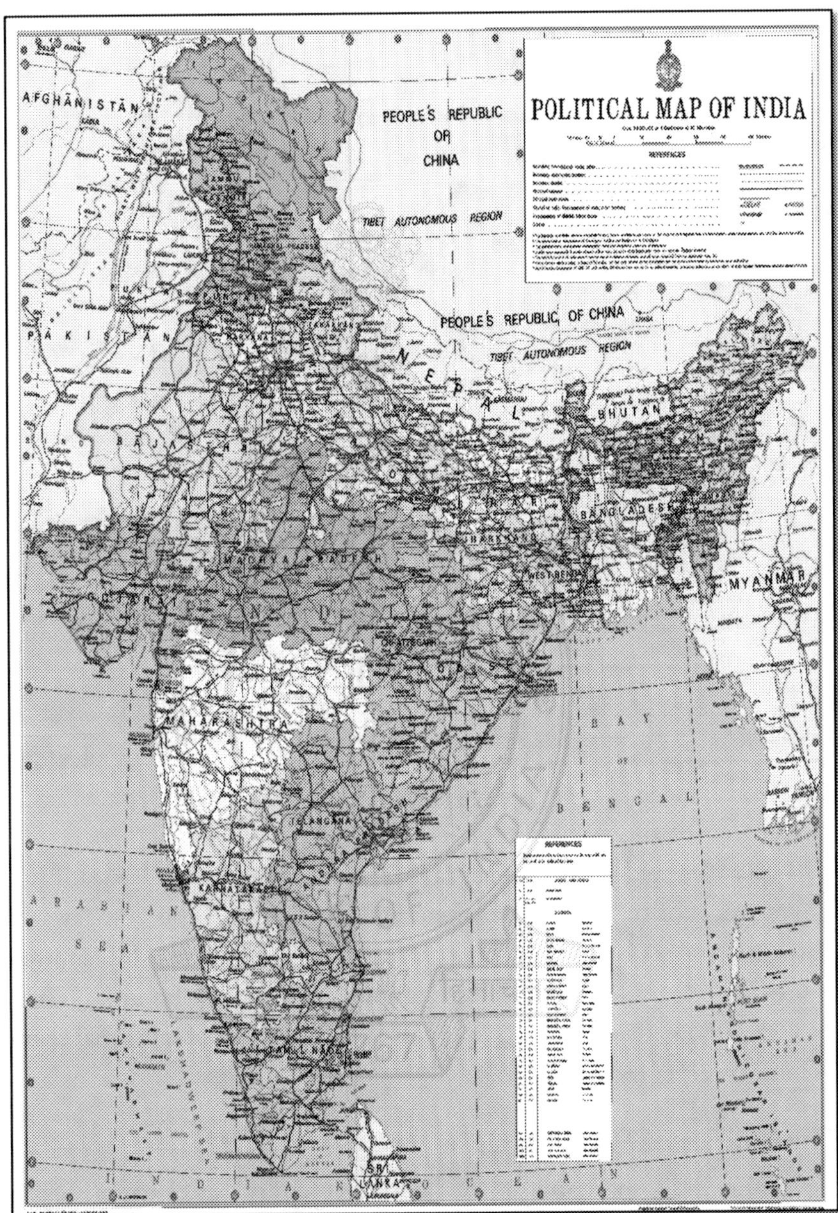

Map 2.5: Political Map of India

Source: Survey of India, Political Map, 9th Edition 2019.

agreeing parties has come to light, the only way to ascertain the correct location of Kali is to examine the existing maps of the period.

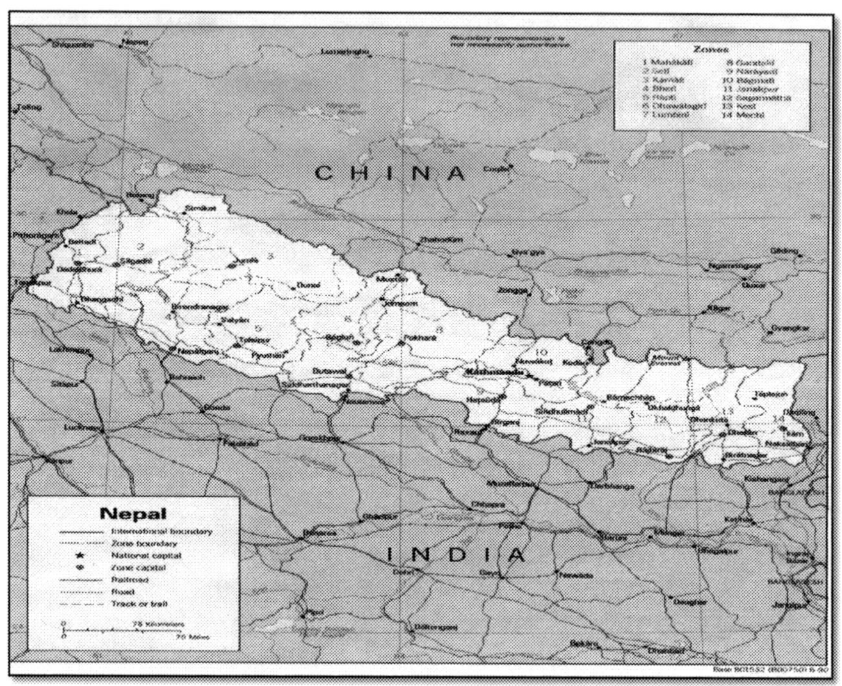

Map 2.6: Map of Nepal[31]

India objected to the cartographic assertion of Nepal. The official spokesperson of the Ministry of External Affairs (MEA) on 20 May said, This unilateral act is not based on historical facts and evidence. It is contrary to the bilateral understanding to resolve the outstanding boundary issues through diplomatic dialogue. Such artificial enlargement of territorial claims will not be accepted by India.[32]

The Politics of Water

Nepal and India share one of the largest geo-hydrological regions called the Ganga-Brahmaputra Basin. Nepal covers a large part of the upper catchment of the sub-basin of the Ganges River. Major rivers of the sub-basin like Mahakali, Karnali, Sapt Gandaki and Sapt Kosi originate from the trans-Himalaya region, cross Nepal and flow southwards to join the Ganga in India, and so are international or trans-boundary in nature.

Though Nepal occupies 13 per cent of the total drainage of the Ganga basin, its contribution to the flow of the Ganga river is much more significant, amounting to about 45 per cent to its average annual flow. In the dry seasons, Nepal's contribution to the total run-off is as much as 70 per cent. These hydrological features bind India and Nepal in a relationship of geographical interdependence and economic complementarities of water resource development.

Although the potential for joint endeavours is considerable, cooperation between these two countries on the issues related to water resource development has not been easy and forthcoming. Their efforts have been heavily influenced by geopolitics; marked by emphasis on historical wrongs (real and perceived), big-small country syndrome, failure in understanding each other's sensitivities, aggressive posture, and negative approach.

A major part of the last century was lost in the process, incurring huge opportunity cost of delay for both countries.[33] Due to the nature of its terrain, only three million hectares of Nepalese Terai land is cultivable of which 2.6 million is cultivated and approximately one million hectares are irrigated. Every year, about 175 billion cubic metres of water flows down into the Ganga. Sixty-seven million hectares of Indian cultivable farm land lies in the Ganga basin of which 20 million is irrigated, Whereas six to eight million Nepalese are sustained in the Terai by this water; the Ganga basin in India sustains a population of 360 million.[34]

Paradoxically, both India and Nepal need to utilise the Ganga basin water resources for their individual requirements. Nepal needs to irrigate an additional two million hectares in the Terai. It needs hydroelectric power, assessed to have a potential of 83,000 MW of which 42,000 MW is economically viable and of which only one per cent has been tapped, as yet.[35]

India requires water for irrigation purposes and to control it to overcome and avoid the yearly deluge which ravages its plains. It needs hydroelectric power to sustain its economic growth. Cheap and available electricity from Nepal will not only be of use to India but will generate foreign exchange and resources to the cash-strapped Nepalese.

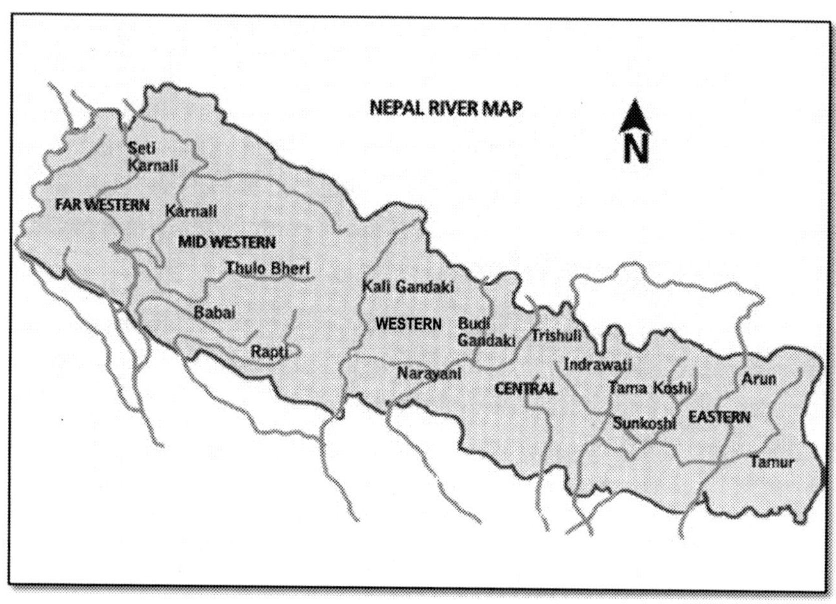

Map 2.7: Nepal River[36]

The Nepalese, historically, have perceived that the management of development of its water resources has been one sided[37] and not a partnership, with India retaining all control during construction as well as in subsequent operations and maintenance. This has contributed to much mistrust as has the apparent lack of transparency. In 1996, India and Nepal had agreed to an integrated development of water resources of the Mahakali River to include the Sarda, Tanakpur and Pancheshwar projects. Despite ratification of sorts by the Nepalese Parliament, opposition towards it continues. It could be that the Nepalese are prisoners of their own hype[38] or that they expect greater Indian concessions in such Himalayan resources, which are essentially required by India.

Interestingly, the earlier Constitution of Nepal, promulgated on 9 November 1990, included a provision in Article 126 that required any resources-sharing agreement to be ratified by a two thirds majority in Parliament, if it was of pervasive, serious and long-term nature.[39] Most Indian projects are thus stalled. On the other hand, no such clearances are taken for Chinese projects or Australian ones (the 750-MW West Seti project is one such case). The draft constitution is also likely to include references of the same.

Issues that need to be considered by both nations are as follows:

(a) Any Indian initiative in terms of providing finances and resources for water and power projects will be based on its requirements to control the flow of water in the monsoons in addition to the advantages in irrigating large tracts and securing electricity.
(b) Joint management of such large projects therefore may be a necessity to counter Indian fears that a purely Nepalese management may not be suited to cater to India's requirements of water management during the monsoons.
(c) The cost of electricity needs to take into consideration the need for suitable remuneration for Nepal and that it should be economically viable for Indians who utilise it.
(d) The negotiations must be transparent.
(e) Involvement of the private industrial sector in Nepal may speed up the agreements on water management.

The two governments have recently been engaged in intensive engagement through the Standing Committee on Inundation Problem (SCIP) on the issue of inundation due to construction of embankments and other structures on both sides of the border. In the case of two inundation issues, the Rasiaval Khurd Lotan Bund bordering Rupandehi district in Nepal and Kaikalwa marginal embankment bordering Banke district of Nepal, a high level technical committee met several times and carried out several joint surveys that did not indicate worsening of the inundation problem due to the embankment construction.[40]

The Power Trading Corporation had signed a Power Purchase Agreement with an Australian company (Snowy Mountain Engineering Corporation), which is developing a 750-MW West Seti hydro power project in Nepal. Nepal has several other small and medium sized project proposals that can be developed by the private sector including companies in India.[41]

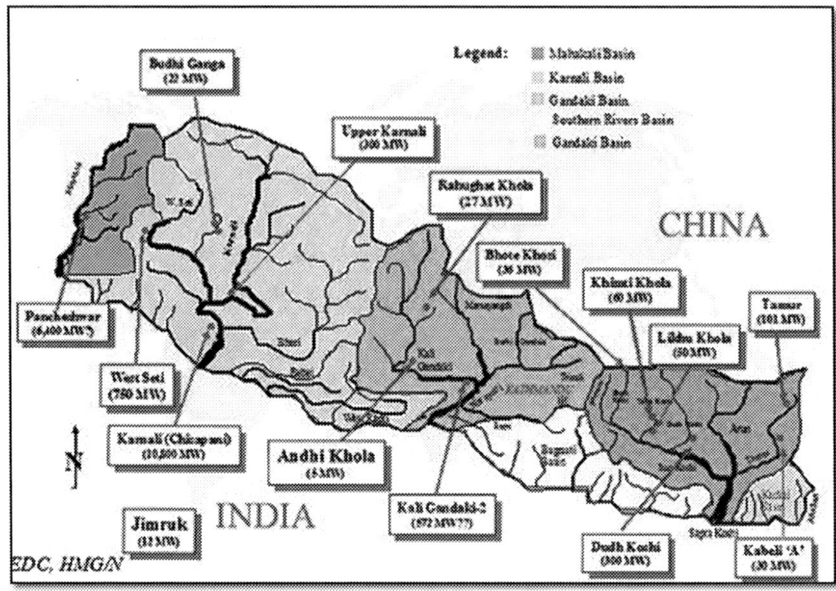

Map 2.8: Rivers of Nepal[42]

Baggage of the Past

Despite huge potentialities and commonalities of objectives, water resource development has faced many setbacks due to political and economic factors that acted against the interests of the two countries. Nepal's complaint about getting an unfair deal in earlier treaties like the Kosi Treaty (1954) and the Gandaki Treaty (1959), cast its shadow over future collaborations. Nepal water resource experts complained about unilateral initiatives of India, nominal and delayed compensations, disregard for Nepal's interest and unequal benefits. These projects created ill feeling and mistrust between two nations leading to a big gap in joint water resource development initiatives. The efforts between the two countries have suffered due to twin factors:

(a) Firstly, policy makers of India for long failed to understand apprehensions of the smaller neighbour. Nepal, sandwiched between two giant nations, has its own world view.

(b) Secondly, Nepal has over-emphasised sovereignty issues. The history of negotiations regarding water projects on Indo-Nepal trans-boundary waters got dominated by controversy primarily due to perception differences and an avoidable blame game instead of technical difficulties.

The Nepalese believe that India is draining Nepal's watershed for its own benefit and have long viewed India as a hegemonic power that arm-twists neighbours for unfair agreements. India, in turn, blames Nepal as suffering from a small country syndrome, imagining non-existent conspiracies and ignoring India's contribution to different sectors of Nepal economy. Further, fragile and unstable political uncertainties in Nepal have also played a role in fuelling anti-Indian sentiments.[43]

Opposition to such projects is mainly instigated by the Maoists/ politicians who prosper in situations of poverty, deprivation, and unemployment which such projects will remove. India, therefore, should address Nepalese fears directly and create assets of great mutual benefit.

India-Nepal Transit and Trade Treaties

The India-Nepal Treaty of Transit (Appendix C) provides for port facilities to Nepal at Kolkata and specifies 15 transit routes between Kolkata and the India-Nepal border. For bilateral trade, 22 entry/exit points are provided along the Indo-Nepal border. The Transit Treaty was renewed in March 2006. The renewed treaty contains liberalized procedures for the transit of Nepalese goods. A Nepalese request for automatic renewal of the treaty for a further seven-year period was accepted. The treaty, however, provides for a termination notice of six months by either side. The Protocol and Memorandum to the treaty containing modalities and other arrangements are to be reviewed every seven years or earlier, if warranted. The renewed treaty and its provisions particularly India's positive response to Nepal's request for its automatic renewal, were well received in Nepal. The transit facility is reviewed/extended on an annual basis.[44]

The first Treaty of Trade and Commerce was signed on 31 July 1950. This had 10 Articles and was of 10 years duration with possible extension or termination clauses. The treaty set the tone for development of economic relations between the two countries.[45]

The treaty provided Nepal with unrestricted imports and exports through India and duty-free transit within India. It provided Nepal with third country access through five designated ports in India. However, it failed on the following counts:

(a) The treaty required Nepal to levy customs duties equal to those levied by India on its import and exports from third countries. It debarred Nepal from price competition, that is, its export levy on exports to India was not to be less than Indian excise duties on similar products. This rationale was not acceptable to the Nepalese psyche because of industrial asymmetry and its need for greater exports.
(b) The treaty provided for common market arrangements between India and Nepal, without, however, explicitly stating it.[46]
(c) Pooling of earned foreign exchange in Reserve Bank of India (RBI) and the general licensing policy.[47]

The year 1989 marked a watershed in Indo-Nepalese relations. Simmering discontent at Nepalese behaviour over the preceding years led to a complete breakdown of bilateral relations and non-renewal of trade and transit agreements.

Some of these irritants that led to this breakdown were as listed below:

(a) Nepal's importing of sizeable quantity of arms and equipment from China.
(b) Nepal playing the China card in infrastructure development in the Terai area leading to India's economic disadvantage.
(c) Inclusion of Indians in list of foreigners contrary to the provisions of the Peace and Friendship Treaty of 1950.
(d) Deprivation of concessions to Indian goods.
(e) Large-scale smuggling due to extensive transit routes.

Nepal was hard hit by this development. Its economy was devastated. The costs of importing oil, coal and essential commodities from third countries were prohibitive. Nepal also learnt the basic fact that China was not suitably placed to assist it economically. Fresh trade and transit treaties were put into effect in 1991 and after five years the trade treaty was once again renegotiated and introduced in December 1996. Liberal concessions were granted to Nepal and it led to a sevenfold increase in exports and a threefold increase in imports. Concessions extended with all good intentions marked a new era in the direction of making SAARC Preferential Trading Arrangement (SAPTA) successful and the consequent free trade area among member nations of the region a reality.[48]

Nepalese goods were given access to the Indian market free of customs duties and quantitative restrictions for all articles manufactured in Nepal. The Nepalese raw material content of 50 per cent, as existing, was waived. However, India asked Nepal's government to ensure that mechanisms were evolved to control the inflow of third country goods through Nepal into India. Re-assembling and repacking of third country goods and labelling them Made in Nepal,[49] to exploit the Indian market, was disallowed.

On small-scale goods, India agreed to extend parity in levy of additional duty, on Nepalese items, equal to effective excise duty on similar Indian products. For large-scale industrial items, India would pay to the Nepal government up to 25 per cent of cost difference against Indian costs so as to make it competitive. It was expected that this remuneration would flow to industrial units in Nepal. India also committed that one-time locked Nepalese containers would not be opened by Indian customs, so as to simplify procedures unless there were reports of contraband being brought in.

It may be said that the renewed treaty was the result of the Gujral Doctrine, which catered to accommodating all neighbours even at our cost. Nepal was unable or even unwilling to plug loopholes in illegal trade. The zero per cent import duty became counterproductive as Nepal re-exported third country goods to India especially Chinese goods. What was essentially meant to boost Nepalese industry only led to personal gains of a few businessmen. Indian small-scale industry has been seriously threatened and affected by this. In 2000, India resorted to non-tariff barriers and in 2001 the countervailing duty (CVD) was introduced on the maximum retail price (earlier introduced as a non-tariff barrier). Though effective, it will also squeeze the economics of Indian investment in Nepal, presently at 35 per cent of Nepal's GDP and 40 per cent of its employment.[50]

The transit treaty was renegotiated and put into effect from 5 January 1999. It overcame earlier lacunae such as that the right to the sea was guaranteed to Nepal as also the existing freedom to transit through India. The duty insurance clause has increased from 0.15 per cent of the value to three per cent. This was put into effect by an amendment to the treaty.[51]

ISI and Terrorism in Nepal

The open and porous Indo-Nepal border runs along five Indian states, that is, Uttaranchal, Uttar Pradesh, Bihar, West Bengal and Sikkim. There are 21 recognised and manned border check points consisting of police, customs and immigration officials. In addition, intelligence and revenue enforcement personnel also man these areas.[52] However, trans-border movements across the long border have grown unchecked especially in the Terai, Naxalbari, Darjeeling and West Sikkim areas.

Islam first came to Nepal in the 18th century. Defeated Indian rulers often found sanctuary along with their followers in the lower reaches of the Himalayan kingdom. Presently with the borders in Rajasthan, Punjab, and Jammu and Kashmir sealed and increasing police pressure in Gujarat and Mumbai, Muslim extremists and ISI have made Nepal their base for undercover operations. Neutral Nepal is an ideal third country conduit for anti-Indian elements, especially due to the ease of entry by air and ground. Particularly, the Muslim population has shown disproportionate growth in Nepal. To some extent, initially, it may be attributable to communal disturbances in the neighbouring states of India. The Muslim population increased by 38.9 per cent in these 10 years. Nearly 96.7 per cent of this Muslim population is confined to the Terai region where they constituted 7.32 percent of the population in 1991.

The Nepalese are not so worried about the increasing number of madrasas, mosques and other Islamic institutions but about the large-scale conversion of Hindus to Islam and Christianity. Consequent to Hindu-Muslim clashes in 1992 and 1994 in Nepalgunj, the Pakistan embassy had advised Muslims in these areas to buy weapons for self-defence.

It is a known fact that certain terrorists and related criminals are engaged in gun-running, narcotics, smuggling and money laundering and using the open border between India and Nepal to infiltrate and cause mayhem within India. Though the Nepalese did have some significant successes and busted some ISI spy rings and apprehended and later extradited Yakub Memon (of the infamous Bombay blast fame) to India in 1994, however subsequently, little has been achieved. Nepal appears to be ignoring the build-up of this terror-related activity within Nepal to target India. This tolerance has encouraged known fundamentalist and terror-funding organizations in Nepal to create a power bloc, driven by inimical Middle East money and related Islamic NGOs.

This menace fuelled by the ISI, in some years will not only seriously erode law and order problems in Nepal but create an inimical, anti-Indian belt along our borders to directly target our heartland, the Indo-Gangetic plains, where India is most sensitive. There is, therefore, the need to carry out some measures to check this menace. Measures suggested are covered under three heads; Indian, Nepalese, and joint measures.

Indian Measures

(a) Strict surveillance of all entry points into Nepal, as well as the airports of Dacca, Karachi, Singapore, and Delhi.

(b) Border sealing to be carried out by para military forces.

(c) Fencing the border should be considered.

(d) Establish military presence in certain hotbeds of ISI activities to counter ISI activities as required on own side of the border.

(e) Raise issue strongly with the Nepalese using all possible means including trade, transit, economic and political to galvanise Nepalese actions and clamp down on ISI agents, conduits, and recruitments.

(f) Closely monitor ISI activities on own side of the border so as to negate any northern side-stepping and seeking safe havens in the Nepalese Terai.

(g) Keep Nepalese authorities informed of all information and data regarding ISI elements.

Nepalese Measures

(a) Close monitoring of all ISI activities in Nepal, identifying areas and causes of subversive activities and removing them with all possible speed.
(b) Monitor and seal foreign funds supporting ISI activities.
(c) Employ political and diplomatic means to curb such activities.

Joint Measures

Reworking the Extradition Treaty to make it more responsive.

(a) Data sharing and exchange of information on a regular basis on ISI agents, sources and activities. New Delhi's concern over Pakistan's use of Nepalese territory for anti-Indian activities has been conveyed by the Minister for External Affairs, Jaswant Singh, during his visit to Nepal in August 2001. The Prime Minister of Nepal, Sher Bahadur Deuba, confirmed that such activity would not be allowed or tolerated from its soil.[53]
(b) Joint patrolling or close coordination at border management. Allow hot pursuit in either country. Joint action will be in the spirit of the 1950 treaty. Towards this end, measures to implement joint activities by way of command, control and communications be organised and resources be made available by India
(c) Establishing hot lines at all levels including district level to coordinate common measures at non-military levels.

Madhesi Movement and India

In geographical terms, Terai means flat land stretching from the foothills of the Himalayan region in the north to the Vindhyachal Parvat (Vindhyachal Mountain) in the south situated in Central India and Nepal. The term Madhesh itself is derived from the Sanskrit word Madhyadesh implying the Gangetic plain and the Vitri Madhesh area bordering India on the southern side and spreading north up to the foothills of the Siwalik Range. The Terai region, which is mostly a flatland, is geographically and culturally distinct from the hills. The Madhesh has historically been part of the larger Mithila region. Most of the affluent of the Terai are educated in India, and the democracy on the other side of the border has kept levels of political awareness high.[54]

According to the population Census of 2001, it occupies 23 per cent of the total area and 48.5 per cent of the population of Nepal. Most of the Terai inhabitants are plains people or Madhesi whose religious traditions, language, caste system, food, style of clothing and other social customs and manners are similar to the people of the Indo-Gangetic plains in the south. Their mother tongues are Maithili, Bhojpuri, Awadhi, Urdu, Hindi and Bengali, and dialects of these languages are used by the Janjati groups. After the unification of Madhesh in Nepal by Prithivi Narayan Shah in 1769, its border was again re-drawn by the Sugauli Treaty concluded between British India and Nepal in 1816. The treaty scattered the people in Madhesh across the border that divides India and Nepal internationally. The Madhesis have ever since been divided till this day.[55]

Area and Population

The total land area in the 20 Terai districts is 34,109 square kilometres which accounts for 23.1 per cent of the country's total area (Table 1). In 2001, 48.4 per cent of the country's total population of 23.2 million lived in the Terai districts with a density of 329 persons/sq. km. The Terai plain and Vitri Madhesh together cover 15.6 per cent of the country's total area.

Exclusion of Madhesh

Social-Cultural Factors

Social exclusion is defined as the inability of the society to keep all groups and individuals within reach of what we expect as a society and the tendency to push vulnerable and difficult individuals in the least populous places.[56]

Education: The literacy level of the Madhesis in Terai (including inner Terai) is only 38.4 per cent as compared to 65.6 per cent for the Pahadi (including Himali) group. The Dalits are the most deprived group of population in Nepal, with only 39.2 per cent literacy. There is, however, substantial difference in the literacy levels between hill Dalits (47.9%) and Terai Dalits (23.4%). Terai Dalits are on the lowest rung of the socio-economic development ladder. Similarly, the literacy rate of the Janjatis of Inner Terai and Terai together is only 50 per cent as compared to 58.7 per cent for Himal and 63.2 per cent for the Hills. The literacy rate of Terai castes (including Muslims and excluding Janjatis and Dalits) is only 35.2 per cent as compared to 72.0 per cent for hill caste groups. Thus, the literacy level of hill castes is more than twice that of Madhesi castes. The average literacy rate of the Pahadi origin groups living in the Terai region is 54.5 per cent, while that of the Terai origin groups population living in the Terai region is 26.4 per cent. The wide gap between the Pahadi and Terai origin populations in the Terai region is a serious matter which warrants immediate attention of policy makers.

Economic Factors

Poverty: People living under the absolute poverty line in Nepal are currently estimated to be 31 per cent. However, about 46 per cent Dalits, 41 per cent Muslims and 33 per cent indigenous Janjati population are below the poverty line. Together these three major ethnic groups form 52.6 per cent of the total Madhesi population. The remaining 47.4 per cent of the Madhesi people have a lower poverty level. The above poverty data indicates that a large proportion of Madhesi households are excluded from mainstream development. Poverty itself is the main factor of exclusion; the poor people could not afford basic education, primary health care, sanitation practices and decent housing.[57] These figures indicate that the Terai districts having higher proportion of Madhesi population have much lower socio-economic index values compared to the districts where hill people are in dominance.

Government and political institutions have been advocating and focusing poverty reduction programmes, mostly in the hills and mountains, and they have been convincing donors that only the hills and mountains have a large number of poor people. It appears that until now politicians, policy makers, decision makers and national planners who are themselves hill origin people have ignored the socio-economic development issues of Madhesh. The fact is that the Madhesi people are not in the right place and their voices are not heard or considered.[58]

Land Ownership: Acquisition of land assets is linked to citizenship issues. Since the knowledge of writing and speaking Nepali language was a clause in the Citizenship Act of the 1960s for obtaining citizenship certificates, it was intentionally formulated to deny citizenship to Madhesis. The Madhesis of Terai, who have been living for several generations, are denied citizenship certificates due to them incompetence in the Nepali language and without citizenship, a land registration deed (lalpurja) is impossible and hence so many Madhesi are landless. Landlessness has become a major problem among the Madhesi community.

A recent report indicates a grave situation particularly in the Dalit, Janjati and Muslim ethnic communities; about 37 per cent of Dalits and 32 per cent of Janjati households do not own agricultural land while 41 per cent of Muslims are landless. About 79 per cent of Mushars, a Dalit community, do not own land; they have the lowest literacy rate of 7.3 per cent.[59]

Economic Exclusion: Three castes/ethnic groups, namely, Brahmins, Chhetris and Newars, have dominated the civil services in Nepal. In 1991, these three castes constituted 36 per cent of the total population in Nepal but occupied 89.2 per cent of positions in the civil services, while the Madhesi community accounted for 32 per cent of the population but occupied only 8.4 per cent of the positions in the civil services.[60]

This indicates that the Madhesi people have been highly discriminated in government services. It is interesting to note that in 1971, these three castes had occupied 89 per cent of the posts in the civil services.[61]

Thus, the pattern of the civil services had not much changed over the past twenty years with Brahmins, Chhetris and Newars dominating the civil services over the years and it is very unlikely that this trend will change in the near future.[62]

These Pahadis, Brahmins and Chhetris control most of the powerful positions and influence the government and other governing institutions. They consider Madhesis as non-Nepali or less Nepali and as its consequence, the latter, gets excluded from high posts. A very low or negligible representation of Madhesis can be seen in constitutional bodies and in high posts/designations – where people make national policies, and are the key decision makers and policy implementers.[63]

Political Factors

Representation in Judiciary: About eight per cent of the total judges of the country are from Madhesi communities whereas the remaining 92 per cent are from hill communities. Participation of judges from Madhesi communities at the Appellate Court is 14.9 per cent, which could be considered a high level of participation compared to 3.7 per cent at district courts.[64]

Electoral Constituencies: The average population per constituency is considerably higher in the Terai districts (127,414) than in the mountain (73,026) and in the hill (109,081) districts. This reduces the number of parliamentarians representing the Terai region where about 96 per cent of the country's total Madhesi people live while increasing their number from the hills and mountains where 82 per cent of the country's total Pahadi people live.[65]

The Madhesis sympathy towards India is more a cultural than political issue, given their centuries-old relationship with the people of India and their desire to maintain it. The Nepalese political parties have not been sympathetic to their plight and discriminate against them, even after the formation of the Democratic Secular Republic of Nepal.

As noted by a former Deputy External Affairs Minister of India, Surendra Pal Singh: As long as the Madhesis keep their cultural links or other types of links with another country, naturally they will be looked upon with suspicion. However, the fact of the matter is that both the hill people and those of Terai origin have a strong cultural affinity with India, apart from property and business interests. Given the rigid positions taken by the major political parties in Nepal over the demands raised by the Madhesi groups, the region will witness some serious ethnic unrest.

India, however, is faced with a dilemma: any constructive attempt by India to salvage the Terai situation is likely to be interpreted as unnecessary intervention in the internal affairs of Nepal and upset its Pahadi constituency whereas passive indifference to developments in Terai will be construed as shirking of Indian responsibility by the Madhesis. India cannot afford to ignore developments in Nepal, especially the discrimination against the people of the Terai region.

Therefore, it is in the interests of both the countries and for the internal cohesion in Nepal, that the people of Nepal, including the Madhesis, settle the issue through dialogue and consensus within the framework of the new Constitution. Similarly, the Madhesis need to conform to the constitutional norms of Nepal. Both the Pahadis and Madhesis should overcome their mutual mistrust and devote themselves to the nation-building process.

Nepal's New Constitution: An Analysis from the Madhesi Perspective

Nepal's new Constitution was promulgated in Kathmandu on 20 September 2015. It failed to satisfy the Madhesis and Tharus who constitute 70 per cent of the Terai population, who regard the formation of seven federal provinces as per the Constitution as grossly unfair to them. Only eight districts in the Terai region, from Saptari in the east to Parsa in the west, have been given the status of a province: the remaining 14 districts are to be joined with the hill districts with the sole purpose of converting the local people into a minority. The Madhesis and Tharu were sidelined in the entire constitution-making process due to prevailing distrust towards them among the mainstream political parties. Of course, the Bijay Kumar Gachhadar-led Madhesi Janadhikar Forum-Democratic was initially involved in the constitution drafting process; but later on, it also had no option but to quit the alliance as its point of view was not entertained.[66]

Effect on India

Instability in Nepal is likely to have an adverse impact on India's political, economic and security interests. Any upheaval in the Terai bodes more ill for India. The anti-Indianism flowing especially from the Madhesi movement will again have an adverse impact on India's economic and security interests in the border region. Since the Terai is closely linked with India, a troubled Terai may affect every major highway, customs point and industrial zone, as well as Nepal's trade with India and other countries. India, however, is faced with a dilemma; any constructive attempt by India to salvage the Terai situation is likely to be interpreted as unnecessary intervention in the internal affairs of Nepal and upset its Pahadi constituency, whereas, passive indifference to developments in Terai will be construed as shirking of Indian responsibility by the Madhesis. India cannot afford to ignore developments in Nepal, and especially the discrimination against the people of the Terai region.[67] Therefore, it is in the interests of both the countries and for internal cohesion in Nepal that the people of Nepal, including the Madhesis, settle the issue through dialogue and consensus within the framework of the new Constitution. Similarly, the Madhesis need to conform to the constitutional norms of Nepal. Both the Pahadis and Madhesis should overcome their mutual mistrust and devote themselves to the nation-building process.[68]

The gains for China will always be disproportionately higher than the losses that India would incur if there is a prolonged crisis in the Madhesh region. At the same time, leaving the Madhesis high and dry in the present situation, when there is a perception in Madhesh that India might reverse its course to placate the leadership in the hill region, could complicate the Nepalese situation. There is a need, therefore, to engage leaders of all political parties and craft another consensus. This can ensure Nepalese unity and integrity at one level and cement India-Nepal ties on the other.

NOTES

1. Ministry of External Affairs, Government of India. Treaty of Peace and Friendship,, 31 July 1950, Kathmandu at http://mea.gov.in/bilateral-documents.htm?dtl/6295/Treaty+of+Peace+and+Friendship accessed on 12 March 2013.
2. Ibid.
3. Chowdhuri, S.R. Monarchy in Nepal, *The Hindu*, 27 July 2001 at http://www.thehindu.com/ 2001/07/27/ stories/05272524.htm accessed on 12 March 2015.
4. Thapliyal, S. *Mutual Security: The case of India-Nepal.* Lancer Publishers, New Delhi, 1998, p. 59.
5. Rajbahak, R.P.*Nepal-India Open Border*, Lancer Publishers Pvt. Ltd., New Delhi, 1992, p. 16.
6. Thapliyal, S. op. cit., p. 49.
7. Nayak, N. India-Nepal Peace and Friendship Treaty (1950): Does it Require Revision? *Strategic Analysis,* vol. 34, issue:4, 2010, pp. 579-593.
8. Ibid.

9. Thakur, S. Nepal to Delhi: Junk sentiment and special ties, *The Telegraph*, 3 May 2008 at https://www.telegraphindia.com/1080503/jsp/nation/story_9219398.jsp accessed on 8 August 2013.
10. India ready to renegotiate 1950 treaty with Nepal, *One India News*, 6 May 2008 at http://news.oneindia.in/2008/05/06/india-ready-to-renegotiate-1950-treaty-with-nepal 1210072316.html accessed on 8 August 2013.
11. Ranjan, K.V. Should the 1950 treaty be scrapped?. *The Hindu*, 3 May 2008 at http://www.thehindu.com/2008/05/03/stories/2008050352481000.html accessed on 8 August 2013.
12. Nepal wont jeopardise any genuine Indian interest, *The Hindu*, 3 September 2011 at http://www.thehindu.com/opinion/interview/article2419048.ece accessed on 8 August 2013.
13. Nayak, N.R. Madhesi Movement in Nepal: Implications for India, (2010), p. 1.
14. Sharma, U.P. (1996). Ecology of the Koshi river in Nepal-India (north Bihar): a typical river ecosystem.
15. Negi, S.S. *Himalayan Rivers, Lakes and Glaciers*, Indus Publishing Co., New Delhi, 1991, p. 82.
16. CIA –The World Factbook, Field Listing-Disputes-international, Produced by CIAs Directorate of Intelligence, United States of America.
17. India's Boundary Disputes with China, Nepal, and Pakistan, *International Boundary Monitor*, 15 May 1998 at http://www.boundaries.com/India.htm accessed on 12 August 2016.
18. Sood, Rakesh. For a reset in India-Nepal relations, *ORF Commentaries,* 29 May 2020, https://www.orfonline.org/research/for-a-reset-in-india-nepal-relations-66997/
19. Kallol Bhattacherjee (2020). Kalapani row: Nepal to deploy more forces on India border, says Foreign Minister Gyawali,, *The Hind*u, 10 May 2020.
20. Kumar, Alok Gupta. Kalapani: A Bone of Contention Between India and Nepal,, IPCS # 422, 17 October 2000.
21. Gupta. *The Context of New-Nepal* (2009).
22. Alok Kumar Gupta. Kalapani: A Bone of Contention Between India and Nepal, 17 October 2000. 422, *IPCS Journal.*
23. Nayak.
24. Ibid.
25. Karki, Sumitra (2020). A view from Kathmandu: Deciphering the Kalapani-Lipulekh conundrum, *Raisina Debate*, ORF, May 2020.
26. Baral, Toya Nath (2018). Border Disputes and Its Impact on Bilateral Relation: A Case of Nepal India International Border Management, vol. 1, no.1, *Nepal Journals Online,* Nepal.
27. Sohini Nayak. India and Nepal's Kalapani border dispute: An explainer, ORF Issue brief and special reports, 29 April 2020.
28. Survey of India. http://www.surveyofindia.gov.in/pages/display/235-political-map-of-india
29. Mohan, Geeta. Kalapani an integral part: Nepal objects inclusion of unresolved territory as part of India in new maps, *India Today*, 7 November 2019.
30. Sood, Rakesh. For a reset in India-Nepal relations, *The Hindu*, May 2020.
31. India's Small Development Project deal in Nepal does not get extension: Report Kathmandu. Financial Express, 6 August 2017.

32. Ministry of External Affairs, Government of India, Official Spokespersons response to media queries on the revised map of Nepal released by Government of Nepal, Ministry of External Affairs, India, 20 May 2020
33. Tiwary, R Indo-Nepal Water Resource Negotiation: Deepening Divide over Border Project (Globalization and Particularism in South Asia, *South Asian Journal*, 2006, p. 11.
34. Rangachari, R. Water Resources Management in India-Nepal Cooperation, In K. Bahadur and M. Lama (eds.), *New Perspective on India-Nepal Relations*, Har-Anand Publication, New Delhi, 1995, p. 263.
35. Ibid.
36. Ibid.
37. Gyawali, D. Himalayan Waters: Between Euphoric Dreams and Ground Realities In K. Bahadur and M. Lama (eds.), *New Perspective on India-Nepal Relations*, Har-Anand Publications, New Delhi, 1995, p. 249.
38. Gyawali, D and Dixit. Mahakali Impasse and Indo-Nepal Water Conflict, *Economic & Political Weekly*, 1999, pp. 553-564.
39. Ibid, p. 560.
40. Ibid.
41. Ibid.
42. Gyawali, D. and Dixit. Mahakali Impasse and Indo-Nepal Water Conflict, *Economic & Political Weekly*, 1999, pp. 553-564.
43. Tiwary, R. Indo-Nepal Water Resource Negotiation at https:// ishuaryal.wordpress.com/ 2016/05/23/ Indo-Nepal-water-resource-negotiation/ accessed on 30 August 2017.
44. Shrestha, G.R. Nepal-India Bilateral Trade Relations: Problems and Prospects,, Research and Information System for the Non-Aligned and Other Developing Countries (RIS), New Delhi, June 2003, pp.27-41.
45. Ibid.
46. Rajbahak, R.P. op. cit., p. 81.
47. Ibid.
48. Katti, V. *Indo-Nepal Trade: Post WTO Dimension,* Kalinga Publishers, New Delhi, 2001, p. 55.
49. Manchanda, R. Neighbours: Business not as usual: India-Nepal trade relations force another round of turbulence, *Frontline*, vol. 18, issue: 8, 2001, pp. 63-64.
50. Ibid., p. 56.
51. Katti. op. cit., p. 56.
52. Mehta, A.K. Problems of Terrorism and Other Illegal Activities on the Indo-Nepal Border: Issues in Effective Border Management, In Ramakant & B.C. Upreti (eds.), *India and Nepal: Aspects of Interdependent Relations*, Kalinga Publications, Delhi, 2001, p. 19.
53. *The Pioneer*. 20 August 2001, New Delhi. athttp://www.dailypioneer.com/ accessed on 31 July 2013.
54. Bhattacharjee, Kallol. Why are India and Nepal fighting over Kalapani? *Indian Express*, 24 May 2020, https://indianexpress.com/article/explained/who-are-the-madhesis-why-are-they-angry/
55. Singh, A.K. Restructuring of Nepali State: A Madheshi Perspective, Nepal Centre for Contemporary Studies, 2004, pp.3-5.
56. Gill, Peter & Paswan Bhola. *In the heart of Nepals Madheshi Movement.* Published by The Wire Publishers New Delhi. (2017), p. 1.

57. ICIMOD (International Centre for Integrated Mountain Development), *New Era*, Nepal, 1997, pp. 1-2.
58. Karna, V.K. Madhesh and Madheshi: A Geographical And Historic Perspective, *Madhesi*, 20 March 2007 at https://madhesi.wordpress.com/2007/03/20/madhesh-and-madheshi-a-geographical-and-historic-perspective/ accessed on 12 April 2016.
59. Shah, S.G.Social Inclusion of Madheshi Community in Nation Building, *Democracy for Nepal*, 21 February 2006, at http://demrepubnepal.blogspot.in/2006/02/govind-shah-social-inclusion-of.html accessed on 12 April 2016.
60. Shah, S.G. op. cit., pp. 15-17.
61. Ibid.
62. Rana, P.S.J.B. *Nepal's Fourth Plan: a Critique*, Yeti Pocket Books, Kathmandu, 1971, pp. 18-19.
63. Singh, A.K. op. cit., p.16.
64. Ibid.
65. Ibid.
66. Jha, H.B. Nepals New Constitution: An Analysis from the Madheshi Perspective, Institute for Defence Studies and Analyses, 24 September 2015 at http:// www.idsa.in/discommends/NepalsNewConstitution_ hbjha_240915 accessed on 12 April 2016.
67. Nayak, N. Nepal: New Strategic Partner of China?, Institute for Defence Studies and Analyses, 30 March 2009 at http://www.idsa.in/idsastrategiccomments/NepalNew Strategic PartnerofChina_NNayak_300309 accessed on 12 April 2016.
68. As Tension Sweeps the Terai Plains, Nepal Tilts Toward China, at http://knowledge.wharton.upenn.edu/public policy accessed on 12 April 2016.

3

Indo-Nepal Military Security Relations

Introduction

Around the middle of the 18th century, the Himalayan region between the Teesta River in the east and the Satluj River in the west was under the control of a large number of independent principalities.[1] It is possible to count at least 60 such principalities, although a complete, authentic list is not yet available. The eastern section of the Himalayan region was less fragmented than the western. It was composed of two small states, Sikkim and Bhutan, which were dissected by numerous rivers, including the Teesta. The territories west of Sikkim, up to the Dudhkosi River, a tributary of the Kosi, were divided into the three comparatively large principalities of Vijayapur, Chaudandi, and Makwanpur. These principalities controlled extensive agricultural and forest areas in the Terai, comprising the modern districts of Jhapa, Morang, Sunsari, Saptari, Siraha, Dhanusha, Mahottari, Bara, Parsa, and Rautahat, while the borders of Vijayapur and Chaudandi also touched Tibet in the north.[2]

The valley of Kathmandu was the centre of three independent states, namely, Kathmandu, Patan, and Bhadgaun.[3] These states also owned territories in the hill areas of the Trishuli River, a tributary of the Gandaki River in the west, and the Dudhkosi in the east. The boundaries of both Kathmandu and Bhadgaun touched Tibet in the north, while in the east they included parts of the modern districts of Kavrepalanchok, Sindhupalchok, and Dolakha.[4] In the west, Nuwakot and Dhading belonged to Kathmandu and Patan, respectively. Patan's disadvantage in not having a direct link with Tibet was compensated by its proximity to the Bhimphedi-Hetauda route leading to the southern plains through the kingdom of Makwanpur. The valley was of great importance from the economic point of view, for it accommodated important trade routes connecting northern India with central Tibet.

Farther west, beyond the Trishuli River, was the Gorkha Kingdom which was destined to bring the whole of the Teesta-Satluj region under its control by the first decade of the 19th century. Unlike most of the principalities of the west, Gorkha has had a recorded history from the time of its establishment in 1559, when Drabya Shah, a prince of the royal house of the adjoining principality of Lamjung, wrested the territory from local tribal chiefs and brought it under the authority of a Hindu king for the first time. Gorkha comprised an area of about 2,500 square kilometres in a triangular area east of Lamjung and Tanahu, with Tibet in the north and the inner Terai region of Chitwan in the south. Lamjung and Tanahu belonged to a cluster of 24 principalities, or Chaubisi, situated between the Marsyangdi River, a tributary of the Gandaki, in the east and the Bheri River, a tributary of the Karnali, in the west.[5] Other important principalities in that region which have affected the course of modern Nepali history during the late 18th century were Kaski, Parbat, and Palpa. Palpa, the biggest and most powerful among the Chaubisi principalities, possessed Butwal and other territories in the western Terai, which it had obtained on lease from the nawab of the Indian state of Awadh.[6] Farther to the west of the Chaubisi states lay another group of states collectively known as Baisi, which included Jumla, Doti, Jajarkot, Salyan, Dullu and Dailekh. Two small states in the mountain region across the Mahakali River, Jauhar and Darma, were also traditionally regarded as constituents of the Baisi group, having once formed parts of the territories of Jumla.

The Himalayan region situated west of the Mahakali River and east of the Jamuna River contained two states, Kumaon and Garhwal. Kumaon had possessed some territory in the Terai,[7] but that territory had come under the control of the nawab of Awadh during the late 1770s. The territories of Garhwal, on the other hand, extended to the Doon Valley, north of the Siwalik. The Jamuna-Satluj region encompassed approximately 14,000 square kilometres but was divided into nearly 34 independent principalities during the late 18th century. Four of these principalities outstripped the others in size and strength, namely, Sirmur, adjoining Garhwal on the west, Hindu, Bilaspur and Besahar to the north. Between Besahar and Bilaspur were situated two groups of tiny principalities collectively known as Barha Thakurai and Atthara Thakurai. Beyond the Satluj River lay the principality of Katoch, which boasted Kangra, the most renowned fort in the Himalayan region.[8] During the latter part of the 18th century, a new state was founded in the Himalayan region in the north of the Indian subcontinent. That state, formed through the expansion of Gorkha, a small principality in the western part of that region, was the forerunner of the modern kingdom of Nepal. The fledgling state faced innumerable trials and challenges in the process of expansion, the most serious being a war with the British East India Company during 1814-16, which resulted in the loss of extensive territories. Only after that did Nepal emerge as an independent state within clearly demarcated boundaries.[9]

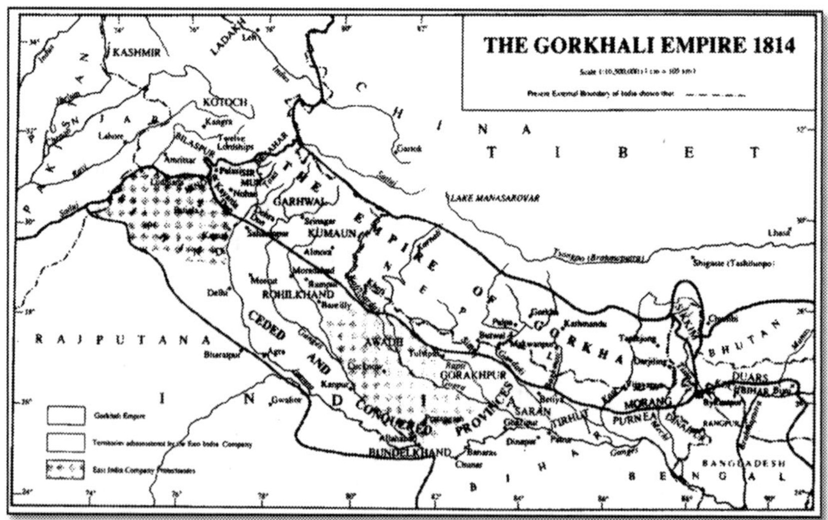

Map 3.1: Map of the Gorkhali Empire 1814[10]

Nepal's Wars in the Kumaon Hills

The Chand dynasty of Kumaon had two rival noble families in court, namely, the Maras and the Phartyals.[11] When the Chand dynasty began fading out, the Phartyals and the Maras were at loggerheads to seize the throne. The Joshis represented the Maras. The Chand family king, Lal Singh Phartyal, overtook the Joshis and positioned his son Moha Singh on the throne, renaming him Mohan Chand, King of Kumaon. The Phartyal and Joshi families began quarrelling and his family, including his son, Harsh Dev, were incarcerated. Obsessed with taking revenge, Harsh Dev spent the next 26 years finding ways to oust Raja Mohan Chand and the entire Phartyal clan from Kumaon. Powerless by himself, Harsh Dev resorted to seeking help. In 1788, Harsh Dev managed to kill Raja Mohan Chand with the help of mercenaries. But Lal Singh Phartyal positioned his nephew, Mahendra Chand, on the throne and Harsh Dev lost again. In 1789, Harsh Dev invited the Gorkha Sena to defeat and expel Raja Mahendra Chand.[12]

In 1790, under the command of General Amar Singh Thapa, distinguished as Badakaji Amar Singh Thapa The Elder, the Gorkha Sena crossed the Mahakali River to Kumaon.[13] Overpowering all resistance, they reached Almora where Harsh Dev joined them providing all support. Almora soon fell to the Gorkhas. Meanwhile, the Gorkhas also received a call for help from Bajhang against Doti, and so a plan was made to conquer Doti, westward of the Mahakali River.[14] In 1790, the Gorkhas attacked Doti and expelled the ruler, Prithvi Pad Shahi (who would later befriend the British against the Gorkhas in the 1814 Battle of Nalapani). The Gorkha conquest over Doti strengthened their kingdom till the banks of the Mahakali River.

After the successful ouster of the Phartyal king of Kumaon in 1790, Harsh Dev now wanted the Gorkha Sena to subjugate Garhwal. He was also to be ceremoniously appointed as the agent of Kumaon by Nepal. This ceremony had to be cancelled since the Gorkha forces received news that China had attacked Nepal, and the troops had to rush back to Kathmandu.

Before the Gorkhas returned, the King of Garhwal, Pradyumna Shah, approached the Gorkhas to formalise a peace and diplomatic accord with Nepal.[15] He would pay an annual tribute, and the Gorkhas would treat Garhwal as a protectorate state. The Gorkhas accepted the proposal. Already discomfited at the cancellation of his appointment ceremony, the dejected Harsh Dev reacted jealously to the confederation of Garhwal and Nepal. While the Gorkha Sena was away, he began a hate campaign, planting seeds of ill-will against the Gorkhalis in the Kumaon-Garhwal region.[16]

In 1795, King Pradyumna Shah stopped paying tribute to Nepal, and, as a result, war was declared on Pradyumna Shah. By this time, the Gorkha army was free from its engagements in Nepal and returned to the Garhwal-Kumaon region, under the command of General Amar Singh Thapa.

In October 1803, the Gorkhali army concentrated 45 companies in Kumaon. Each company had 200 soldiers bringing the total to 9,000 soldiers. Except for the superior and junior officers who were Nepalese, most of the soldiers were Kumaonis, Rohillas, Mohammedans, Garhwalis, and the like. Such a congregation of mercenary soldiers was a usual practice with armies at that time. Crossing the Pindari River, the Gorkhas reached the banks of the Mandakini River. King Pradyumna Shah retreated towards Saharanpur with Amar Singh Thapa close on his heels. Finally, the two forces clashed at Khurbura on 8 June 1804, near Dehradun. Unfortunately for Garhwal, on the first day itself, Pradyumna Shah was fatally wounded, following which his son Parakram Shah abandoned the battlefield. The Garhwali defences fell, and it was a victory for the Gorkhas. Amar Singh Thapa arranged for Pradyumna Shah's body to be wrapped in an expensive shawl and under full escort, carried it to Haridwar for a cremation befitting a king.[17]

One of Pradyumna Shah's sons, Pritam Shah was taken as a hostage to Nepal (where he was married to the daughter of Bam Shah, the Gorkha Governor of Kumaon), while another, Sudarshan Shah, was granted asylum by the British with whom he allied to assault the Gorkhas later. Amar Singh Thapa returned to the west, and the Gorkhas gained 54 Garhwal forts, including Langur Garhi, Lobha, Chandpur Garhi, Jableshwar, Badhangarhi, Sirgur Garhi, Dewalgarh, Nawalgarh, Chilgarh, Naithana,

Khurkhuri, and others during this campaign. Dehradun also now came under Nepal.[18]

The Gorkha Sena, after the Garhwal and Kumaon campaigns, moved further away from Nepal. Their encounters brought them face to face with many of the greatest armies in the region, including that of Maharaja Ranjit Singh and Raja Sansar Chand II. Maharaja Ranjit Singh ruled the Kangra Fort territory under administration from Lahore. Across the Sutlej River, the Gorkhas ruled from Arki, capital of Baghal State (whose ruling family had been displaced to Ropar) over their territories till the boundaries of the Garhwal and Kumaon kingdoms.

The army of the East India Company at that time comprised a large number of Scottish and Irish mercenaries. Controlling India necessitated a larger regular and standing army. The army also provided great ancillary opportunities for blacksmiths, horse breeders, gold and silversmiths, tailors, gun mechanics, and the like. Further, they borrowed many ideas from the armies of the many Indian kingdoms that they had fought against and won. The pomp and glory of the imperial army was borrowed from Tipu Sultan's army, the Marathas and other great armies. One of the best ideas they incorporated from the armies of various Indian rulers was the use of elephants to haul heavy guns atop hilltops during the Anglo-Gorkha wars. The tame, strong and trainable pachyderms were a useful graduation from native porters or mules to carry their loads. Another advantage the British had been acquiring were troops starting with plainsmen such as the buccaneers and purbiyas (fighters from the eastern Gangetic Plain).[19] Since the entire region consisted of big and small separate kingdoms that were perpetually at war with each other, it was not difficult to get soldiers from one kingdom to battle against their arch enemies of the other. The purbiyas had no reason not to fight against buccaneers and so on and so forth. The Indian sentiment of oneness would be exhibited much later when, for the first time, they became slaves under British India and realised that to gain independence, they had to unite as one. The British colonisation of the multitude of Indian states inadvertently played a role in bringing about the sensitivity of bringing a feeling of being a single people from the north, south, east, and west under a region larger than ever.[20]

Anglo-Nepal Wars

The East India Company had a skirmish with Nepal during the office of Governor-General Gilbert Elliot, the Earl of Minto. It was over a disputed tract of land in the Terai region. By the time Francis Rawdon-Hastings, the Earl of Moira, took over as British Governor-General of India from 4 October 1813, matters had snowballed to a situation where Hastings found it inevitable to declare war. The debacle over a wasteland at Butwal Terai, also called the Hastings' Bluff, was instigated. The growing stature of the Gorkha Sena of a hitherto unknown kingdom of Nepal had reached challenging heights for the British. By 1804, Nepal's western section included Kumaon-Garhwal extending across the hill states of Sirmour, Nalagarh (Hindur), Bilaspur and Bushahr including the petty states of Bahra Thakurai and Athara Thakurai till the eastern territory of southern Sikkim. The East India Company, on the other hand, had taken over Hindustan and more. Nepal's clash with the Company began as their territories started overlapping each other. With new acquisitions, old disputes were also inherited, particularly in the Terai area, which ran across the state of Oudh where the Company had started establishing protectorates under its administration. The Terai Arc, which forms the southern strip of Nepal, was a no-man's land where only local natives could survive. For Nepal, the Terai was not only a source of agriculture but also a habitat for wild animals like tigers, rhinos and elephants. Kathmandu-dwellers owned land there from where they derived income from the crops while the royals visited for personal or diplomatic hunting trips. For the same reasons, the Terai was also of interest to the Company.[21]

In 1795, Lord Cornwallis had assured the Raja of Nepal of defining the borders along Morang and Purnea districts, but the work had not materialised since records were inaccurate and the cultivators did not permit revenue collectors to enter their territories. This region was an exceedingly hostile area with no Company functionary wanting to go there for any legal landmarking. In 1804, when General Amar Singh Thapa conquered Palpa, he expected continuance of rents from Butwal near Gorakhpur. But when Nepalese officers went to Butwal to collect the same, they were shocked to know that the Nawab of Oudh had ceded Gorakhpur to the

Company. The Nepalese offer to retain Butwal with rental to the Company was rejected. A year passed, and as the Company did not press its claim, the Nepalese continued to visit the Butwal villages, with an interpretation that as long as they paid rent to the local zamindars (who also received it), they were at liberty to continue farming. Eventually, the Company revenue collectors accused Nepal of unlawful land occupation. In 1806, Bhimsen Thapa believed the Company was a threat and built a fort at Kheri (east of the Kali River) between Oudh and the hills.[22] In 1811, the Magistrate of Bareilly reported that the Gorkhas had built a fort in an area which had been assessed as ceded and was a part of the conquered provinces of the Company and therefore no revenues had been actualised. Discussions on these border issues were held in Calcutta, and it was decided that Nepal had no rights on the border areas till they were finalised. Earlier, in 1765, the Company had acquired rights over Bettiah with hundreds of villages, of which Nepal claimed the lowlands of Makwanpur. The Raja of Bettiah, now a Company zamindar, took the law into his hands and sent armed mercenaries to murder the Nepalese Subba or Governor there. Nepal's appeal for justice to the Patna and Saran courts was responded with the verdict that the zamindar could not be blamed since the Nepalese Subba was guilty of unlawful possession. Nepal, displeased at the favouritism shown to the Raja, consented to a joint commission to inspect the border issue, claiming ownership of 22 more Saran villages besides the ones in dispute.[23] This border dispute brought Nepal in conflict with the Company and the need to tame Nepal was considered. With Nepal's expansion over the west and east, it was seen as an expansionist power with a formidable presence towards the Northwest Frontier.[24]

Any conflict across the Terai had to be seasonal, as it was endurable only for a restricted time. During the monsoon months from April to October, fatal malaria fever was deadly in the Terai. The ominous campaign of 1766 led by Captain George Kinloch through the Terai to Kathmandu was remembered.[25] The idea of one decisive battle was too perilous contemplating the Gorkhas agility in their country. Nepal's long, narrow and horizontal shape was useful to British war strategists. It would have to be pierced at various points simultaneously like a worm being pinned down with a four-pronged fork. Governor-General Hastings planned a campaign, dividing his forces into separate and simultaneous assaults. Fighting at several places over a prolonged stretch and period would break the Gorkha defences stretched over extended ranges. The veteran Gorkha Commander, General Amar Singh Thapa, and the capital at Kathmandu were the cardinal targets the British were gunning for. Amar Singh had to be kept away from Kathmandu, and the two blocked from contact at any point. Two columns were assigned to assault Amar Singh's stronghold in the western Himalayas. Another two would attack from the south of Nepal. By October 1814, merely a few months after the last skirmish at Butwal, the British columns were in position at the four points of assault. The Gorkhas, on the other hand, were not able to complete their preparations in the time that Hastings had expeditiously drawn up.

On 31 October 1814, the British column led by Major General Robert Rollo Gillespie attacked the Gorkha stockade called the Khalanga Fort commanded by Balbhadra Kunwar. Gillespie was killed on the first day. The Gorkhas put up such a robust fight that the British side had to resort to blocking their clandestine water supply to defeat them. The staunch Gorkha defence, hit by lack of water, ultimately crumbled. Balbhadra and his men evacuated the fortress and sped westwards to Jaithak in Sirmour. On 30 November 1814, when British troops entered the fort, they found dead or dying Gorkhas. Major General Gabriel Martindell with his troops then moved towards Jaithak.[26]

The Treaty of Sugauli between Nepal and the East India Company was signed on 2 December 1815.[27] Of the two transcripts of the Treaty signed, one went to Governor-General Hastings and the other to King Girvan Yuddha Bikram Shah Dev for ratification. Governor-General Hastings endorsed his transcript with great relief. The loan of rupees two crores that he had taken from the Nawab of Oudh for the war could now be taken care of. He had been under flak from the Board of Directors for the colossal war expense. Now he planned to recompense half the loan amount by giving the Terai on the Oudh border to the Nawab, with much of Nepal's territories in the west remaining in his possession. Nepal was granted only 15 days to ratify the treaty but was not ready to give up without another fight. Nepal did not ratify the treaty, and the Treaty of Sugauli did not return from Kathmandu with ratification, and the deadline ended. General Amar Singh Thapa who had been called to Kathmandu to endorse the treaty, had protested against the inclusion of Article 4 which stated, "With a view to indemnify the Chiefs and Bharadars of the State of Nepal, whose interests will suffer by the alienation of the lands ceded by the foregoing Article, the British Government agrees to settle pensions to the aggregate amount of two lakhs of rupees per annum on such Chiefs as may be selected by the Rajah of Nipal, and in the proportions which the Rajah may fix."

As soon as the selection is made, Sunnuds shall be granted under the seal and signature of the Governor-General for the pensions respectively.[28] It meant that chosen Nepalese would be allowed to retain jagirs or pensions in the Terai. Amar Singh Thapa was against any Nepalese being pensioners or jagirdars under the British government as it meant they would still be puppets under British rule. He insisted that there should be no grey area and prevailed upon all not to consent to such clauses. Lieutenant Colonel Paris Bradshaw agreed to amend the Treaty and confer the estates in the Terai west up to River Rapti, permanently to the Nepalese. On 28 December 1815, Chandrashekhar Upadhyaya and Pandit Gajaraj Mishra returned to Kathmandu to bring the Treaty duly ratified.

By this time, Governor-General Hastings had appointed a new Political Agent and Military Commander to resume the Treaty talks. On 25 January 1816, the relationship of the East India Company and Nepal was in its third year; when Major General David Ochterlony assumed charge of military preparations to not only capture the forts of Makwanpur but also attack Kathmandu if the Nepalese did not ratify the Treaty. On 27 January 1816, when Pandit Gajaraj Mishra arrived at Sugauli from Kathmandu without the ratified Treaty, he was told to apprise his government that all negotiations had ceased and war declared. On 27 January 1816, a year after he led his campaign against General Amar Singh Thapa from Nalagarh in the west, Ochterlony was at it again, this time from the Terai, close to Kathmandu.[29] Nine kilometres from the periphery of the Terai, the little hamlet of Balwi, at the edge of Saran, bustled with activity as British troops congregated in numbers never seen before. Thousands of soldiers marched in with artillery comprising guns and cannons, elephants and all kinds of support personnel. The planned points of attack were the three forts at Hethauda, Makwanpur and Harcharpur.

Major General Ochterlony with four brigades consisting of 20,000 men and 83 guns would target Makwanpur.[30] On Ochterlony's left, the column led by Major General John Sullivan Wood with 5,000 men and artillery was to advance from the Terai towards Palpa and Tansen. On Wood's left, Colonel Jasper Nicolls, along with Lieutenant Colonel William Gardner, would lead 6,500 men with 20 field guns. Lieutenant Colonel Adams was to advance from Kumaon to the Gorkha position in the west. On 3 February 1816, British troops were back to heaving, chopping, blasting and clearing paths for their guns on elephants again, through the 300 forests of the Terai and up the hills towards the extremely formidable Bichakori Pass.

On 14 February 1816, Ochterlony and his men began negotiating the arduous climb up cliff face of Bichakori Pass. They clung on to shrubs, branches and rocks, whatever they could hold on to, hauling their baggage with ropes. It took them 25 hours to accomplish this herculean task. Ochterlony marched on westwards to Hethauda, crossing the Karra River. He camped there for a week till Colonel Burnet and his troops caught up with him. The Raja or Chogyal of Sikkim offered Tibetan soldiers and full co-operation to Major Barré Latter for his campaign against Nepal's strongholds in southern Sikkim. Latter already had 35,000 regulars and 100 pieces of artillery. After marching eastwards across the Kosi River, Latter reached Titalia, where he added 2,000 Tibetan soldiers. They marched the distance of 370 kilometres from the Kosi River to the Gorkha fort at Nagri which was well defended. Surrounding the fort, Latter laid siege to it and tried unsuccessfully to persuade the governor of the fort, Jayanti Khatri, to surrender.[31]

Map 3.2: Map of Nepal[32]

This Nepal-East India Company war was a terrible ordeal for Nepal. It resulted in the loss of approximately half of Nepalese territory. However, the conflict also manifested and proved to the British the fighting mettle of the Nepalese under severely adverse circumstances.

Earlier, the Nepali invasion of Tibet in 1855 had also resulted in disaster for the kingdom of Nepal and once again resulted in great losses once China intervened. The result was the signing of the Treaty of Thapathali, concluded in March 1856, which forced Nepal to acknowledge the special status of China in Tibet and also committed Nepal to assisting Tibet in the event of any foreign intrusion. In the 19th century, Nepal aligned itself with the British Raj in India and supported its invasion of Tibet in 1908. When China sought to claim Tibet in 1910, Nepal sided with Tibet and Britain and broke relations with China after Tibet drove Chinese forces out in 1911.[33]

The 1950-1951 invasion of Tibet by the People's Liberation Army resulted in significant changes in the Chinese relationship with Nepal. China ordered restrictions on the entry of Nepalese pilgrims and contacts with Tibet and increased its support for the Communist Party of Nepal, which was opposed to the Nepalese monarchy.[34] Mao repeatedly said from

1950 onwards that Taiwan, Tibet, and the Hainan Islands were Chinese territories and would be re-possessed. The predominant trait in this claim was the advent of maps showing large parts of Korea, Indo-China, Mongolia, Burma, Malaysia, Eastern Turkestan, India, Tibet, Nepal, Sikkim, and Bhutan as Chinese territories. In fact, Mao repeatedly stated publicly, that Tibet was the palm of a hand, with its five fingers being Leach, Sikkim, Nepal, Bhutan, and the North East Frontier Agency.[35]

This statement of Mao worried King Tribhuvan of Nepal who invited the Indian Military Mission (IMM) to Nepal for reorganizing and modernising his army. Before King Tribhuvan's takeover, Nepal had no regular army or soldiers. They were kept part-time and when not on duty followed other professions. Periodically, they were called for parades in Kathmandu. This army was ill-equipped and ill-paid.[36]

The IMM arrived at Kathmandu on 28 February 1952, and was tasked to assist in the reorganization of the Nepali Army, formulating defence plans against internal and external threats, and improving intelligence and administrative establishments. The IMM was considered a sell-out to India, by various political parties including the B.P. Koirala faction of the Nepalese Congress Party. The IMM comprised a Major General assisted by 20 Indian army officers. In December 1953, its strength was a total of 197 all ranks. On its recommendations, by April 1952, the Royal Nepalese Army (RNA) was downsized from 25,000 ill-organised, ill-paid and undisciplined soldiers to 6,000 better trained and equipped ones.[37]

Meanwhile, in September 1951, 17 check posts were established, with Nepalese concurrence, along Nepal's northern borders with China.[38] These were manned jointly by 75 Indian technicians and RNA personnel. In mid-1958, the King asked India to withdraw the IMM.[39] As a result, India agreed to reduce its strength to 23 in all and retain it under the name of Indian Military Training and Advisory Group (IMTAG). On 5 June 1969, the Nepalese Prime Minister asked for the withdrawal of the check posts and IMTAG and stressed that Nepal could not compromise its sovereignty for India's so-called security.[40] The withdrawal of military personnel was completed by August 1970. In practice, Nepal remains in close touch with India in matters of defence and security.

In 1965, consequent to the arms agreement, India was required to supply arms, ammunition and equipment to the entire RNA of 17,000 personnel, comprising four re-organised brigades. It catered for replacement of existing weapons as well as training.[41] Military relations soured with the withdrawal of the IMTAG. After the restoration of amicable relations, post-1989 crisis, the Nepalese sought India's help in raising large-scale military formations by reorganising the existing army from its battalions and independent companies into brigades and divisions. The Maoist rebellion in Nepal forced the Government of Nepal to relook at the equipping of its army and make it capable of fighting the Maoists. Once again, Nepal requested assistance from India and a host of other nations including the USA, the UK, and China, the EU, and Pakistan, all of whom reacted in various ways and provided Nepal with diverse military equipment. From India, under a 70 per cent assistance scheme, and through a series of defence-purchase negotiations, the RNA received more than 26,000 weapons of various kinds including 21,000 Indian-made INSAS rifles, 81 and 51 mm mortars and other military hardware including land mines, detonators, safety fuses and time pencils. India also provided four advanced light helicopters. Post the Jan Andolan and under admonition of the Government of Nepal, India suspended military aid and supply of lethal equipment but continued with the supply of non-lethal weapons to include 216 light vehicles, 154 heavy vehicles, including 58 trucks of 7.5 ton capacity, 67 trucks of 2.5 ton capacity, four ambulances, and 25 multi-purpose armoured vehicles, among others.[42]

The Comprehensive Peace Agreement between the government and the then Maoist rebels stopped both parties from procuring arms and ammunition until the completion of the peace process.[43] After the conclusion of the peace process and with the integration of the former Maoist combatants into the Nepal Army, the government of Nepal wrote to all countries having diplomatic relations stating that there was no obstruction for procurement of arms and ammunition.[44]

Nepal continues to request arms assistance/weapons from India under the Nepal-India Peace and Friendship Treaty of 1950. Article 5 of the said treaty mentions that Nepal was free to import arms from any third country but needed to consult the Indian government before doing so. This clause Nepal continues to disregard.[45]

This clause has remained a divisive and debated issue among the leaders, experts and analysts and has often been termed as unequal while some politicians have maintained that this treaty compelled Nepal to depend on India. Several people want a re-examination of the treaty while some have been demanding that the accord be scrapped in the changed geopolitical scenario.

Since the reinstatement of democracy, post the Jan Andolan in Nepal, military relations and cooperation between the two countries gradually improved. Likewise, India's concern and ascendency, after Nepal's peace process, has increased dramatically.

Military Relations between India and Nepal Post-Independence

At the time of Independence, there were 10 Gorkha Regiments in the Indian Army. Although Pakistan also made a bid for the surplus Gorkha regiments, they did not press their claim, and, of course, Nepal could not be expected to go along with that claim.[46] Six Gorkha Regiments were earmarked for the Indian Army and four for the British Army.[47] It was also decided that a referendum be held in all Gorkha units for the Gorkha soldier to give his choice for service in the Indian or the British Army. Till 1947, the British had debarred Indians from joining the officer cadre of Gorkha Regiment. Even when Gorkha soldiers from Gorkha Regiments got promoted to commissioned ranks, they were not accommodated in Gorkha Regiments. They were posted to different Indian Regiments. British officers fervently believed that as the Gorkha soldiers had been serving only under them and they had no contact with Indian officers, the result of the referendum among Gorkha soldiers was a foregone conclusion. But the results of the referendum came as a great shock to them. Well over 90 per cent of Gorkha soldiers opted for service with the Indian Army. Non-optees from Gorkha Regiments earmarked for service with the British Army were drafted into newly-raised battalions of the Gorkha Regiment allotted to the Indian Army.[48] A new Gorkha Regiment, namely the 11th Gorkha Rifles, was raised for the soldiers who opted for India.[49] After Independence,

Indian-origin army officers were posted to Gorkha units for the first time. It took a few months for these units to settle down with a completely new set of officers. Thus, in the initial months of the 1947-48 war in Jammu and Kashmir, there was no participation of Gorkha units. However, later, they more than made up for it in Kashmir.[50] These Gorkha Rifles regiments later distinguished themselves in the assault on the 10,000-foot Pir Kanthi Hill and during the epic battle of Zojila.[51]

During the advance to Kargil, a Nepali origin junior commissioned officer, Subedar Harka Bahadur Gurung, swam across the icy-cold swift flowing Shingo River in winter to enable a rope bridge to be built. Even today the concrete bridge later constructed at that site bears his name. There were many gallantry awards of Maha Vir Chakras and Vir Chakras earned by Gorkha units in Kashmir. They also earned an Ashok Chakra, the highest gallantry award in peace during the police action in Hyderabad.[52] In every war fought by the Indian Army after Independence, the Gorkhas have played a gallant role. They have earned several Param Vir Chakras, the highest award for gallantry.

Since 1965, both the countries confer the title of Honorary General on each other's Army Chief. The two armies exchange goodwill visits since 1950, when the then Chief of the Indian Army, General K.M. Cariappa, visited Nepal. Since then, 21 Indian Army Chiefs visited Nepal while 16 Nepal Army Chiefs have visited their southern neighbour.[53] The relationship between the Nepal Army and the Indian Army is excellent. A large number of officers and men undergo professional military courses in India. Further, a large number also have close relations (both serving and retired) with their kith and kin who serve/served in the Indian Army.[54]

Traditionally, the Chief of the Army Staff (COAS) of the Nepal Army visits India at the earliest after assumption of the post, during which he is conferred with the rank of an Honorary General of the Indian Army by the President of India. In 2016, Nepal Army Chief, General Rajendra Chettri, visited India and was conferred the rank of Honorary General in the Indian Army and the Indian Army Chief, General Bipin Rawat, was conferred this rank in the Nepal Army in 2017.[55]

In 1995, India had in principle accepted the request of the Government of Nepal to assist the then RNA in its modernisation and re-organisation process. During 2004-2007, defence stores worth INR 212,858,333 were provided to the Nepal Army (NA), gratis. Apart from the stores supplied under the Modernisation Programme, the NA also purchases defence stores on payment. Due to recent political changes in Nepal, the quantum of supply of defence stores supplied to the NA has considerably reduced.[56]

Based on an agreement during the Seventh Nepal-India Bilateral Consultative Group on Security, the two countries commenced joint training at platoon level (30 men each) in 2011. The first two joint exercises focused primarily on jungle warfare and counter-insurgency operations. Troops shared their experiences and exhibited skill sets during joint training at Counter Insurgency and Jungle Warfare School at Vairangate in Mizoram and a similar school at Amlekhganj in Nepal. This level of joint training was upgraded to company level in 2012.

Subsequently, the Indian and Nepali armies crossed another historic milestone when a battalion from each of the countries took part in a combined training programme to ensure inter-operability in the disaster-prone region of Uttarakhand. The Indo-Nepal Joint Military Training Exercise, Surya Kiran-V, was conducted at Pithoragarh in Uttarakhand from 23 September to 6 October 2013. This was the first of the battalion-level combined training exercises between the two countries, and at least 400 soldiers from each army participated at Pithoragarh where the focus was on Disaster Response in the geological disaster-prone zones of the Himalayas.[57] In February 2016, the Ninth Indo-Nepal Combined Battalion Level Military Training Exercise Surya Kiran was conducted at Pithoragarh. During this exercise, the Indian and Nepali armies trained together and shared their experiences of counter-terrorism operations and jungle warfare in mountain terrain.[58]

These Surya Kiran series of exercises are bi-annual events which are conducted alternatively in Nepal and India. The aim of these combined training exercises is to enhance interoperability between Indian and Nepali army units. The training also focuses on humanitarian aid and disaster relief (HADR) including medical and aviation support. Both the armies stand to benefit mutually from these shared experiences, and this combined training, mutual interaction and sharing of experiences between both the countries further invigorates the continuing historical military and strategic ties, giving a further fillip to the bilateral relations and existing strong bonding between both countries.[59]

Integration of Maoist Combatants into the Nepal Army

The integration of Maoist combatants into the Nepal Army post the revolution was the most contentious and emotive issue.[60] According to the agreement on monitoring of the management of arms and armies between the Nepal Government and the Maoists on 8 December 2006, the United Nations Mission in Nepal (UNMIN) had identified 19,602 Maoist combatants. I had the opportunity of visiting some of these camps in both eastern and western Nepal during my tenure as the Defence Attaché in the Indian Embassy in Kathmandu. Initially, it was found that the Maoists had registered 32,250 cadres, a much larger number than what we were aware of their assumed strength. Though I repeatedly brought this to the notice of the UNMIN officials, they insisted on accepting them as cadres of the Maoists and placing these unverified cadres in the 28 cantonments nominated by the UNMIN.[61] Later, after being forced to carry out a more detailed screening process, 19,602 cadres were found eligible to be treated as combatants, and they were transferred to seven camps.[62] These too were much higher than the known strength of the Maoists, which was between 5,500 and 6,000.

Around 90 per cent of these so-called combatants living in the seven UNMIN supervised camps hailed from rural areas of both eastern and western Nepal. During the frequent visits to rural areas of Nepal on pension payment duties, I often visited these camps. It was observed that the military training capability of these cadres was negligible, and when questioned in detail, they revealed that they had been coerced by the Maoists to live in the camps and, in addition, the Maoists had offered them a stipend, which was eventually paid by the Government of Nepal along with rations.[63] These cadres were unmotivated, and many of them had earlier wanted to join the Indian Army or the Nepal Army and in its absence, mainly due to the lack of employment opportunities, joined the Maoists. For the open rallies conducted by the Indian Army subsequently in Nepal, stringent checks were insisted upon and due to the lack of law and order and I recommended shifting of the recruitment camps to Gorakhpur near the Indo-Nepal border.[64] Since these cadres were living in the designated camps since November 2007, they had not undergone any training programme either for military integration (MI) or Civilian Integration (CI). UNMIN was only mandated to provide technical support to the Constituent Assembly (CA) elections and monitoring the peace process.[65] There had been no change in this mandate.

Later, many of these cadres, once they realised they would not be recruited in the Nepal Army due to a detailed verification process using a mix of UNMIN officials and ex-soldiers of the Indian Army that was initiated by me, deserted these camps and very few known cadres remained there. In fact, from the inhabitants of these camps, the Maoists milked many of them for their newly-raised organisation called the Young Communist League (YCL). However, I felt many of these young men and women were innocent victims in a larger game plan of the Maoists to increase their cadres and show greater strength and as a consequence retain a better negotiation posture.[66]

The November 2006 Comprehensive Peace Agreement (CPA), was not as comprehensive as its name implied. It was vague on the future of the two armies and, just as damaging, silent on the question of militias and demilitarisation. Inter-party committees met only sporadically; there were no effective mechanisms to monitor the many commitments that held the deal together.[67]

The Nepal Army (NA) held the view that the lack of conventional training of Maoist combatants would have a serious effect on its professional standards. General Rookmangud Katawal, the COAS of the Nepal Army during the cease-fire, had gone on record to state that though he was fully committed to supporting the ongoing peace process and the CPA, he strongly felt that there were clear recruitment rules framed by a legitimate government which laid down the regular army recruitment norms, on who could and could not be recruited. Further, he felt that the NA would accept only those recruits who met international recruitment norms and who had been verified in detail.[68]

Former Prime Minister, the late G.P. Koirala, who was the architect of the peace process, had pointedly opposed reintegration clearly stating, "We cannot allow the Maoists to integrate the radical communist indoctrinated People's Liberation Army (PLA) cadres and any attempt to integrate the armies would result in a Nepalese bloodbath. We cannot allow the Maoists to transform Nepal into a Cuba or a North Korea."[69]

According to another Nepali Congress leader, Shovakar Parajuli, the Maoist leadership designated Nanda Kishore Pun as chief of the PLA after Prime Minister Pushpa Kamal Dahal relinquished the position in August 2008. Parajuli stated, "We suspect that the Maoists have received support from China in this regard. Other parties are silent, but we object to it." He also claimed that the Maoists were planning to send Pun to China where he would undergo a nine-month higher defence course. Parajuli felt this is a part of the Maoist covert strategy to prove that Pun meets internationally-accepted standards to hold the post of Chief of the Nepal Army.

The Maoists on the other hand argued that since their militia possessed military skills rather than academic qualifications, this should be the criterion rather than any other aspect, and since they claim that their cadres were involved in a 15-year war with the then RNA, they had adequate combat experience and should be given equal positions.

It was envisaged at that time by the leadership of the NA that this Maoist insistence on military skills and not education as the criterion was a ploy when it came to promotions and would especially be problematic while integrating the middle-level leadership of the PLA. Treating academically under-qualified commanders of the PLA at par with well-trained officers of the NA would fan resentment among the existing NA leadership.[70] Since the NA and the PLA had different doctrines, organisational structures, and widely divergent political backgrounds, their integration would, if permitted, especially in the officer ranks, in all probability be a tortuous and difficult process.

Finally, in October 2012, six years after the formal end of the civil war, Nepal's peace process concluded with the integration of a little over 1,450 former Maoist fighters into the Nepal Army. The cantonments where the former combatants of the Maoist People's Liberation Army resided closed down and Maoist weapons were handed over to the NA under state control, and the PLA ceased to exist, ending the state of one country, two armies.[71]

This final phase of the integration process saw 1,388 combatants who had opted for integration pass through the NA-conducted selection examinations and joined the army at the soldier level. Seventy-five other former Maoist fighters who had cleared the written exam to join the NA at the officer level underwent a nine-month training course, and soldiers a seven-month course, in addition to both sets further undergoing an additional three-month bridge course.[72]

In early 2007, about 32,000 individuals had initially registered in the camps. But the UNMIN verified only 19,602 of them as combatants and disqualified over 4,000 persons for being under-age or joining the Maoist army after the ceasefire began. The disqualified were discharged from the cantonments in early 2010.[73]

In November 2011, a seven-point agreement was signed between the parties, which stipulated that a maximum of 6,500 former combatants could be integrated into a specially-created general directorate under the NA. In the first phase of regrouping, over 7,000 combatants opted to retire with cash packages while over 9,000 opted for integration. But in subsequent rounds, this number steadily dipped, and finally, around 1,600 combatants and 116 officer-level former fighters chose to go through selection tests. In April 2012, the NA took charge of the cantonments as well as containers that included over 3,000 Maoist weapons which were transported to various army centres.[74]

Minendra Rijal, a member of the special committee for the supervision, integration, and rehabilitation of former combatants, highlighted the key challenge ahead. He stated, "It is now important that there be no relationship between the Maoist party and those former fighters who have joined the Army; they must see themselves like any other soldier. At the same time, the Nepal Army too must not discriminate against those who have been integrated. That will be the yardstick for successful integration."[75]

Of the 1,463 former combatants who qualified for integration into the NA, 1,420 graduated from the Nepal Military Academy in 2013.

Seventy-five ex-PLA commanders are already serving in the NA as officers. The new graduates were deployed in the National Development and Security Directorate, specially formed to accommodate the former combatants who enjoy a 33 per cent quota in the general directorate. The Nepal Chief of Army Staff in 2015 directed that former Maoist soldiers, who had integrated into the military, would also be allowed to serve in peacekeeping duties in the Nepal Army deployed overseas in UN assignments under a quota system for integrated combatants. The first batch of former combatants participated in peacekeeping missions in Lebanon, Congo and Darfur in 2016.[76]

Origin of Indian Army's Gorkha Soldiers, a Force Multiplier

By 1947, Gorkhas had served as irregular or regular soldiers in the British Indian Army for 132 years. The original four battalions, recruited from deserters and prisoners taken during the Anglo-Nepal war in 1815, with many Garhwalis and Kumaonis among them, had expanded fivefold in peacetime and more than tenfold in the recent war.

Nepal Clans Recruited by the Indian Army

From a multitude of clans in Nepal, the following clans were selected by the Indian Army for recruitment into its Gorkha Regiments: Magars, Gurungs, Khas-Chhetris, Rais, and Limbus, from Nepal and India.[77] A brief on each of these clans are as given here.

The Magars

The Magars constitute the greatest number of Gorkha recruits. Surnames: Thapa, Ale (Aalay), Rana, Budhathoki, Roka, Gharti, Sinjali and Pun (Poon) with Sen, Singh or Bahadur as a middle name. There are about 700 sub-clans of the Magars.[78] Traditionally, their family names are categorised according to Magar Kura speakers (Ale, Thapa, Rana, Sinjali), Khamkura/ Magarpang speakers (Bura, Gharti, Roka, Pun, Jhankri) and Kaike speakers (Tarali Magars of Dolpa/Budha, Gharti, Rokaya, Jhankri). Many surnames are the same as the Khas Chhetris.[89]

Historically, Magar kings such King Aramundi killed Kashmir's King

Jayapida (782-813 CE), while another, King Mukunda Sen of Palpa and Butwal, in 1100 CE, attacked the valley of Nepal. The other Magar kings were King Sintu Pati Sen, King Gaja Laxman Singh of Makawanpur Gadhi, and King Mansingh Khadka, the Magar-king of Gorkha (till 27 September 1559 CE).[80]

Ancient Magar kingdoms in the west consisted of two groups: Athaara Magarath or 18 kingdoms of Magars located west of the Kali Gandaki River and called Kham Magars. The Baarah Magarath or 12 kingdoms of Magars comprise Argha, Khanchi, Gulmi, Isma, Musikot, Ghiring, Rising, Bhirkot, Paiyun, Garhu, Dhor and Satahu, and spoke Magarkura. The Ale, Thapa, Sinjali and Rana Magars hail from the Baarah Magarath. In the east, Magars ruled in southern Sikkim, until displaced by the Chogyal's army from Tibet in the 18th century. Sir Joseph Dalton Hooker, British botanist and explorer who conducted a scientific exploration in Sikkim in 1848-49, stated that the Magars, a tribe in Nepal, living west of River Arun, were actually aborigines of Sikkim. They had been driven out by the Lepchas westward towards the region of the Limbu. Further, wherever the Magars settled, they constructed jongs (forts or castles in Magar phraseology) and established their authority forming small independent principalities in several parts of Sikkim.[81] Places like Magarjong (Mangsari), Berthang Berfok, Kamrang and Kateng in the Sikkim/Darjeeling Hills are believed to be locations of the early Magar jongs. Of the 13 Gorkhas who were awarded the Victoria Cross, five were Magar Gorkhas – Rifleman Kulbir Thapa in 1915, Rifleman Karan Bahadur Rana in 1918, Subedar Lal Bahadur Thapa in 1943, Rifleman Tul Bahadur Pun and Subedar Netra Bahadur Thapa in 1944.[82]

The Gurungs

Surnames: Gurung, Ghale, Ghatane, Lama, Lamichhane. The Gurungs have been clubbed with the Magars in five Gorkha regiments, due to social affinity, inter-marriages in the regimental Gorkha community.[83] The ancient birthplace of the Gurung clan lies in the district of Ghandruk, north of Pokhara, Nepal, from where their name originated. The Gurung clan is composed of two sections: the Charjaat or four sub-sections: Ghale, Ghatane, Lama and Lamichhane; and the Solahjaat composed of 16 sub-sections. With the traditionalists, there still exists the Gurung dharma, which is shamanistic. Three Gurung soldiers received the Victoria Cross, Rifleman Thaman Gurung in 1944, Rifleman Bhanbhagta Gurung in 1945 and Rifleman Lachhiman Gurung in 1945, all from Nepal.[84]

Khas Chhetris & Thakuris

Surnames: Karki, Khadka, Basnet, Bista, Adhikari, Kharel, Kandel, Mahat, Khatri, Rana, Chand, Malla, Bohra, Shahi, Silwal, Parajuli, Budhathoki, Pandey, Ghimire, Baniya, Bhandari, Burha, Burathoki, Bharti, Khandka, Kunwar, Manjhi, Mahat, Rawat, Roka and Thapa. The homeland of the Khas or Khasiya community stretched across from the mountains of Kashgar (China), Kashmir (Khash-mir) to Bhutan;[85] also mentioned in pristine Hindu writings as the region between the Nepal valley and Kashmir. The Khas were non-Vedic Aryans and were influenced by Buddhism. They introduced Hinduism within the Magar community and were the first ethnic clan to embrace Hinduism. The Khas community referred to themselves as Bahun, Bhakuni, Bhhetri, or Bhakuri. Even the so-called socially humble castes such as Damai (tailors and musicians), Kami (blacksmiths), Sarkis (tanners and cobblers) and Gaines (wandering minstrels) are of Khas origin. Since the Khas tribe was considered to be a tribal shudra, the Khas warriors began looking for a name to remove them from the shudra tag.[86]

Khas-Kura: According to an ancient Nepali legend, a 13th century Magar king called Nag Raja or Langha (villages from Central Nepal) Raja, encouraged inter-breeding of the Langha Magars and the Khas race. What evolved was the Dias-Kura, which became the Nepali language. Khas Chhetris, the warrior caste, were those who in 1850 after Prime Minister Jang Bahadur Rana returned from England, began calling themselves Chhetris (Nepali translation of Kshatriyas warriors in the Hindu caste system). Some Chhetri clans also have a racial inheritance from the Rajput migrants from Hindustan. Surnames harmonious to roles are Adhikari (functionary) or Khadka (sword-bearer), Bisht (distinguished), Bogati (kings special messengers), Karki (revenue officer) and Kunwar (prince). Some are Ekthariyas (born of Khas women and Rajput males from India) while others are Matwala Alas (progeny of Khas males and Magar or Gurung females). The Matwala Alas Chhetris from the Karnali region who share Thapa as their last name with Magars, do not wear the Janai or the sacred thread. The majority of senior Nepalese officers of the Gorkha Sena were Chhetris. Khas Chhetri Rifleman Sher Bahadur Thapa received the Victoria Cross in 1944.[87]

Kirati Rais

Surname: Rai (deduced from Raya, or Raja) of the Khumbu region belonged to the Kirati union of Limbu, Yakkha, Dhimal and Sunuwar ethnic groups. The Kiratis contain the Sunuwars, Khambu (also known as Rai), Limbu and Yakkha (Dewan), along with Bantawa, Chamling, Sampang, Dumi, Jerung, Kulung, Khaling, Lohurung, Mewahang, Rakhali, Thulung, Tamla, Tilung, Yakkha, Yamphu and Jero, Rai and Dewan. The Kiratis are a very large, native Himalayan race, extending from Nepal to India, Burma (now Myanmar) and beyond. Their very ancient religion and culture influenced Nepali Hinduism. Kirati King Yalambar, had conquered Kathmandu valley, the central Nepal region, extending his realm from the east of the Teesta River in Bhutan to River Trisuli in the west. By 200 CE, the Licchavis routed the last Kirati king, and drove the Kiratis eastwards towards the Dooars, Assam, Burma, Tibet and Yunnan (China). The Kiratis in north Bihar, north Bengal and Assam are called the Mech people. Despite suffering much displacement, evidence of their heritage exists in unusually faraway locations. Rifleman (acting Naik) Agansing Rai from Nepal, received the Victoria Cross in 1944.[88]

Kirati-Limbus

Hailing from the east, the Limbus have emerged from the Kirati race. The Limbus have a very ancient and distinct heritage of hundreds of clans. Historically, belonging to an executive body called Limbuvan, the people were called Limbus. Subba is a title granted to a village head. Their flag has an upper blue band implying water and sky, a central white band for air and peace, and a lower red band representing earth and the pure bloodline of the Limbus. The sun in the centre denotes their spiritual customs and life. Lance-Corporal Ram Bahadur Limbu (post-1947 10th Gurkha Rifles) received the Victoria Cross in 1965.[89]

The Gorkha Brigade was an elite regiment within the Indian Army, with a fighting record second to none and had won no less than 10 of the 26 Victoria Crosses awarded to other ranks of the Indian Army during the Second World War, though Gorkha battalions comprised only about a fifth of the total number of Indian Army infantry units.

In the context of the Indian independence, however, the fate of the Gorkha Brigade was very much a play within a play. The division of ten regiments of Nepali soldiers between the British and Indian armies scarcely merited comparison with the violence and huge displacement of vast swathes of population caused by the partition of the subcontinent.

Field Marshal Claude Auchinleck's concern for the Gorkhas (as a young subaltern in the Indian Army he almost joined the 1/5th Royal Gurkha Rifles) and for Britain's staunchest wartime ally, Nepal, as well as his strategic thinking about Britain's post-war commitments, may have led him momentarily to overlook India's vital interests. At least, this seems to have been the view of General Mosley Mayne at the India Office in Whitehall, who wrote to Lieutenant General Archibald Edward Nye on Boxing Day 1945:

> "I feel that before HMG (His Majesty's Government) attempts to snap up all the available Gurkha troops, the Indian Government of tomorrow should be given an opportunity of lodging a demand for, at any rate, some of them. From the political aspect, friendly co-operation and interdependence between India and Nepal and from the fighting efficiency of the Indian defence services, I feel that it would be a pity if Gurkhas were entirely excluded from the Indian Army; and until very recently Auchinleck thought so too."

Auchinleck may have been influenced by some of his senior Generals; the most intransigent of whom was Lieutenant General Francis Tuker, the GOC-in-C, Eastern Command. While Tuker accepted that the Indian Army, to as great an extent as was feasible, had to be Indianized, he had no doubt whatever that Britain should take all 20 regular battalions of the Gurkha Brigade, for its whole outlook was British, and it was at that time bound to the British Crown rather than to any Indian Government of the past, present or future. This bald assertion ignores the fact that the entire

Indian Army, not just the Gurkha Brigade, was at that time bound to the British Crown; that would not prevent it from being Indianized.

The communal riots of February 1946 in Calcutta, which the army had the responsibility of suppressing, made it clear that not just that the subcontinent would be partitioned, but that the two states of India would be enemies. Communalism was the reality, and everything else, including independence, was subsidiary. Even in an independent India, the British felt, if the Army were to survive, then it would only survive if it were regrouped into its communal classes.

Auchinleck went to Nepal prior to independence, and realised that it was willing to allow the continued recruitment of Gorkhas into the Indian Army, should the future Indian Government wish to retain the Nepali soldiers. When Auchinleck raised the possibility of the Gorkhas being employed directly by the British Government as part of an imperial strategic reserve in the Far East and elsewhere, the King was positive to his proposals. As stated, "Of the two alternatives ... there is no doubt whatever that they would prefer the latter."

Nepal Prime Minister Juddha Shumsher Jung Bahadur Rana's successor, Padma Shumsher Jung Bahadur Rana, had accepted that Gorkhas would serve in the future Indian Army, and probably in the British Army too and that a negotiating team consisting of an official War Office mission and Indian Government representatives would visit Nepal to settle the issue.

The War Office had sanctioned the permanent employment of eight battalions of Gorkhas and it was contemplating the possibility of asking for several more, perhaps all of the pre-war battalions, though it was reluctant to enter into a long-term engagement stating unless it is essential in the negotiations with Nepal, would prefer not to put a definite term of years to its bid.

In 1945, a committee was formed to study and recommend the reorganization of the Indian Army, in which Brigadier K.M. Cariappa was a member. Besides other issues of a standing peacetime post World War army of India, capable of wartime expansion, the perspective of Gorkha units of the Imperial Army was also discussed. On 28 March 1945, the following guidelines and assumptions for the Reorganisation Committee (India) were laid down for the Gorkha Regiments of the Indian Army:

(a) Gorkha units would be available to the Indian Army as in the past.
(b) They will not be available for the Indian Army, though Nepalese manpower might be available for the Empire as a whole as and when required.
(c) That at a fairly early date India will receive some form of self-government and will enter into treaty relations by which the responsibility for the defence of the India and Nepal would remain with the UK.
(d) That the Indian Government would wish to fill the officer ranks of the Indian Army with Indians as early as possible.[90]

In April 1945, Auchinleck endorsed the idea of Britain employing Gorkhas for its Far Eastern garrisons and advised that the British Government should include as many Gorkha battalions as possible in its strategic reserve, all 20 perhaps, if they could be employed in the Middle East as well as in the Far East. He followed it up by writing to the Vice-Chief of Imperial General Staff, Lieutenant General Archibald Edward Nye, that any plan to take Gorkhas must not be regarded as a temporary arrangement, but as a reasonably permanent commitment.[91]

Auchinleck further drew two extreme scenarios somewhere in between which the actual decision might be: There will be plenty of proven fighting material within India, and there will be stiff competition for the privilege to serve in the Indian Armed Forces, as there was before the war. In such a case, politically it would be impracticable for a national government to recruit foreigners and thus take bread away from the mouths of Indians.[92]

However, the interim Indian Government appreciated that to retain the continuity of the Indian Army, and ensure a good relationship with Nepal and its effectiveness, India must continue to hold permanently, some Gorkha units during peacetime. Further, since time immemorial India and Indians did not consider Nepal and Nepalis as foreigners. A large percentage of the population felt that the destinies of India and Nepal were like their geography and culture, inter-dependent and interlinked. Therefore, they advised India to continue her cordial relations with Nepal, and retain these fine Gorkha soldiers, and continue recruitment as hither-to-fore.[93] If a final solution lay between the above extremes, then India may retain these Gorkha soldiers, but in lesser numbers. This act would in all probability result in the demobilisation of certain units, resulting in surplus trained manpower in Nepal. Nepal's King also conveyed that he would very much wish that this manpower of trained soldiers remains employed, as his Kingdom's economy greatly depended upon the remunerations that soldiers of the Gurkha regiments sent back to Nepal. As Britain was likely to face manpower shortages and would in all probability have to keep some forces in the Far East for some time to come, it was conveyed that she must retain these Gorkha soldiers for her overseas garrison commitments.[94]

It is to the credit of the Gorkha units that during the 1947-48 war with Pakistan, and the infiltration of Pakistani Invaders in Kashmir, the valour, dedication and fighting skills displayed by these soldiers at Zoji La, Jhangar, Poonch, Uri, Kargil, and Leh, to name a few actions, was in keeping with their reputation. It also proved that Indian officers, including the newly-promoted Gorkha officers, were as good if not better than the British officers.

The performance of the Gorkhas during the 1962 Operations, especially at Chushul and Namka Chu, further proved their loyalty, fighting spirit and devotion to duty. The expansion of the Indian Army post the 1962 War, resulted in a few more raisings within the Gorkha regiments, for which Nepal agreed to allow additional recruitment. Again, during the 1965 War, Gorkha units fought shoulder to shoulder with their counterparts and gave a telling blow to the Pakistani Army. It was very heartening that on learning on the radio about the start of the war, a large number of Gorkha reservists from Nepal rejoined their units without waiting for recall notices. The performance of the Gorkha regiments during the 1971 War, in Op Pawan, on UN Missions and in CI Ops in Jammu and Kashmir and the North-East, the Siachen Glacier, in 1999 in Kargil, and in fact in all the battlefields of the frontiers of India continues to be outstanding. In 2023, a Gorkha unit of the Indian Army, 3/5 Gorkha Rifles, representing the country secured gold at the prestigious Cambrian Patrol Competition held in the UK. The team competed against over a hundred teams from across the globe in a competition known as a gruelling ultimate test of human endurance, teamwork, training and skill.

Economic Aspects of Recruiting Soldiers from Nepal

The recruitment of the soldiers who are not Indian citizens is a phenomenon which has no parallel in modern times and is of great benefit to both, Nepal and India. There are a great many reasons why this connection should be continued. Recruitment of Gorkhas in the Indian Army is of great economic advantage to Nepal, and its cessation would produce widespread distress and discontent.[95] For the last 200 years, the 1751-km border between Nepal and India has been peaceful. However, if the recruitment of these soldiers were to cease, then, with the resultant economic dislocation and lack of outlet for the energies of a warlike and adventurous population, India might well be faced with a new and troublesome frontier problem. Thus, in return for the money which flows into Nepal from India as pension and pay, India receives a guarantee of peace along her international border with Nepal. Forty-two units of the finest soldiers are an asset to any country, however well provided for in manpower resources.

Retired Nepali soldiers also get pensions like their Indian counterparts, and according to 2017 figures, 39,000 Nepali soldiers are serving in the Indian Army, while 125,000 ex-servicemen and 17,000 widows draw pensions from India.[96] Notably, Nepali citizens come to India without hindrance for work, and that is a relationship not equalled anywhere between any two countries in the world.

The soldiers and pensioners also provide a well-disciplined population to Nepal, adding to its trained workforce pool. The children of soldiers serving in India receive good schooling, healthcare and practical training, which prepare them for a better future. Families of the soldiers also develop skills for better child care, education and health. Due to these reasons, Nepali soldiers, pensioners and their families are very well respected not only in India but also in their villages at home.

Notably, the Indian Army not only sends pension teams, often on foot, to distribute pensions and welfare grants in inaccessible areas but also sends medical and dental teams to far-flung areas, which provide free medical care to the retirees.[97]

As for the future recruitment of Gorkhas, the wastage rate of these units is approximately 3-4 per cent per year, and with the present pay and allowances, no one wants to go home without completing his full service. Also, after retirement, Nepal domiciled troops prefer a civil job in India, especially as they can hone their civil skills at the Gorkha Resettlement Training Unit (GRTU), Dehradun, while in service. Besides, in any case, they prefer to stay in India because of better facilities for themselves and their families, generally given by the Indian Army. Nonetheless, despite the welcome given to Gorkha soldiers, it is up to the Nepali government to take certain decisions. India may still raise Gorkha units from among those settled in India. In any case, as there are 50 candidates on an average for every vacancy of a soldier, India will not have any dearth of voluntary troops.[98]

For these committed and wonderful soldiers, India too plays a role in ensuring their continued welfare and well-being and has always been proud to have Nepalese as soldiers in her defence forces. She has made every effort to ensure that they are looked after and cared for in their twilight years. As of now, over 1.25 lakh ex-servicemen who served India in her various armed forces reside in Nepal and a further 40,000 continue to serve. To ensure their and their families well-being, the Government of India established the Indian Ex-Servicemen Welfare Organization in Nepal (IEWON) which functions within the Embassy of India under the chairmanship of the Ambassador of India to Nepal and the Defence Attaché.[99]

After India's independence, the responsibility of pension payment was taken over by the Indian Embassy. The first Military Attaché posted in 1949 took over the responsibilities after that. In 1950, some 300 disabled ex-servicemen drawing their pension from Pokhara Mal Adda (equivalent to a district treasury) petitioned the Ambassador that they had not received their pensions for the last two years. The Military Attaché was tasked to set up a temporary camp at Pokhara so that these ex-servicemen could get their dues. Thus, the concept of pension payment camps in the interior areas came into being as it ensured timely payment of pension near the homes of the pensioner saving their money, time and effort to come to collect their pensions. This unique concept of temporary camps was established at Pokhara in 1955 and Dhankuta in 1959. These were converted into permanent pension-paying offices in 1960. The Dhankuta camp then shifted to Dharan in 1968. Presently the Embassy also conducts 36 seasonal pension paying camps annually in the interior of Nepal all over the middle hills, for the convenience of our ex-servicemen.[100]

Since I was India's Defence Attaché from 2004 to 2007, I was, amongst my other duties, responsible for paying pension to pensioners of the Indian Army, the Assam Rifles, the Special Bureau, civilian employees of various state governments and an assorted mix of their ex-Nepali origin government employees. The Military Pension Branch that I led, along with its offices at Pokhara and Dharan caters to more than one 1,25,500 defence, para-military and civil pensioners who have opted to draw their pensions in Nepal. Apart from pension payment, our officers, during these camps, ensure that all the requirements of the pensioners regarding medical, educational scholarships, army group insurance claims, and the like, are dealt with under the concept of a single window thereby obviating the need for pensioners to report at different places. Along with the pension payments, these camps are also utilized for medical outreach programs wherein mobile medical teams from the Indian Army visit Nepal and screen all pensioners and their families along with the dispensing of medicines in the form of an annual medical pack that contained commonly needed medicines for common ailments like headache, flu and fever. These medical teams are of great value and very popular in the continuation and enhancement of goodwill between India and Nepal, and I was continuously requested by the pensioners to increase their outreach during my tenure as the Defence Attaché in the Embassy of India.[101]

Over the last five years, pension disbursed to defence, and civil pensioners who retired from India has been enormous and its direct contribution to the coffers of Nepal is a major stabilising economic force for an underdeveloped country like Nepal and was of an approximate value of INR 11,000 crores, directly paid as pensions to our soldiers, and directly benefitting over 10 lakh Nepali citizens. With this pension payment and the medical outreach and various welfare programmes, there is a continuation of the issue of allegiance to India and the reinforcement of the age-old concept of *namak khana* and loyalty that these old soldiers and their families felt and continue to feel about India.[102]

As mentioned earlier, along with these medical teams, the Government of India also launched the Ex-Servicemen Contributory Health Scheme (ECHS) which was a flagship welfare scheme of the Government of India, launched in April 2003 for all Indian Armed Forces ex-servicemen in India. This was further extended to our Nepal domiciled Indian defence pensioners and their dependents to ensure timely and specialised medical treatment to Nepal domiciled ex-servicemen and their dependents.[103]

The scheme aimed to provide quality healthcare to ex-servicemen (ESM) pensioners and their dependents through a network of ECHS polyclinics and civil empanelled/government hospitals spread across the country and was structured to provide cashless treatment, as far as possible, to its beneficiaries. Also, three polyclinics, one each at Kathmandu, Pokhara and Dharan, were operationalised and are now functional since mid-April 2014 with locally hired medical staff.

Post-independence, the Government of India assumed the responsibility to pay pensions to Nepali-origin Gorkha soldiers who had served in the undivided Indian Army pre-independence. Thus, approximately 30,000 service documents of non-effective Nepal-domiciled Gorkha soldiers were handed over to the Chancery of the Embassy of India, Kathmandu (Nepal) by the British Legation at Kathmandu. The documents were then handed over to the Military Pension Branch in 1955-56. The Record Office in Kathmandu was established in 1960 primarily to attend to the pension claims of our ex-servicemen and maintenance of their 30,000 documents. This Record Office at the Indian Embassy, Kathmandu, is now responsible for the maintenance of approximately 86,000 service documents, in addition to thousands of pension-related cases which increased manifold as a result of the decision of the Government of India to grant family pension to all pre-1964 retirees, 100 per cent endorsement of family pension in respect of pre-1989 retirees, restoration of family pension to liberalized and special family pension awardees and various revisions of pension consequent to the award of the 6th Central Pay Commission.[104] Accordingly, The Record Office in Kathmandu functions for Nepal-domiciled Gorkha soldiers of the Indian Army who are drawing a pension from various pension disbursement agencies in Nepal. The functions of the Record Office in Kathmandu, which is the only one of its type in a foreign country, are more complex than those of all other non-effective Record Offices in India. Apart from its duties like any non-effective Record Office in India, the Record Office in Kathmandu is vested with the authority to investigate and project the genuine family pension claims to the pension sanctioning authority in India vide Paragraph 174 of the Regulations for the Army 1987.[105]

The Origin of the Defence Wing in Nepal dates back to the Tripartite Agreement signed between the representatives of the Governments of UK, India and Nepal on 9 November 1947. The then Nepal Prime Minister, Field Marshal Padma Shumsher Jung Bahadur Rana agreed to maintain the Gorkha connection with the British and Indian armies. The Indian Army has maintained this Agreement in letter and spirit to this day and Gorkhas from Nepal continue to be recruited into the Indian Army. The Defence Wing under the Defence Attaché comprises the offices of the Defence Attaché, Welfare Branch, Military Pension Branch, Record Office and ECHS Branch at Kathmandu and the Pension Paying Offices at Pokhara and Dharan. The Defence Wing has a total strength of nine officers, 46 India-based staff and 187 locally employed civilian staff.[106]

Apart from exercising operational and administrative control over all establishments of the Defence Wing in Nepal, the duties of the Defence Attaché of the Indian Army include:

(a) *Indo-Nepal Defence Cooperation Aspects:* These include, inter alia, training of the Nepalese Army personnel at Indian military establishments and provisioning, sale and repair of all defence-related equipment. In addition, assistance during disasters.[107]

(b) Latest information on issues such as development of strategic infrastructure (i.e., roads, bridges, airfields, railways) in Nepal and regional areas, and keeping abreast with defence cooperation with other countries. It also includes issues that may affect serving Gorkha soldiers of the Indian Army, such as subversive activities by hostile intelligence agencies/organisations.[108]

(c) *Ex-Servicemen (ESM) Related Aspects:* Ensure correct functioning of all branches/offices related to Gorkha ESM.

India has always been proud to have Nepalese as soldiers in her defence forces and is making every effort to ensure that they are looked after and cared for in their twilight years. As stated earlier, approximately 1.25 lakh Nepal Domiciled Gorkha (NDG) Ex-Servicemen (ESM) and civilian pensioners residing in Nepal. The welfare of ESM is undertaken in the remotest areas of Nepal where our brave personnel settle down to lead a peaceful and contented retired life. It has been a constant endeavour to reach out to all our pensioners in their respective areas of domicile. To this effect, the Indian Embassy in Kathmandu, through its Defence Wing, exercises control over 22 district soldier boards (DSBs) functioning in various locations in Nepal, from Baitadi in the west to Ilam in the east.[109] The Welfare Branch which came into existence in the early 1950s has effectively transformed itself as per the temporary welfare aspirations of our Nepali Domicile Gorkha pensioners.[110]

History of the Military Pension Branch of the Indian Embassy, Kathmandu

The Gorkhas were first recruited into the Indian Army in 1815. Until 1949, pension payment was carried out by the Chancery. The pensioners strength then was only about 8,000. In 1949, the responsibility for disbursement of pension to Indian military pensioners were handed over to the Military Attaché. Due to the ever-increasing strength of pensioners, the Military Pension Paying Branch (MPB) was established in Nepal in 1955. Later, in 1960, the responsibility for disbursement of pension to civilian pensioners was also completely handed over to the Military Attaché. The Military Pension Branch comprises of headquarters at Kathmandu and Pension Paying Offices (PPOs) at Kathmandu, Pokhara and Dharan. All these establishments are looked after by a serving Gorkha Regiment officer each, functioning under the Defence Attaché. The headquarters at Kathmandu is responsible for the overall functioning, rulings/policies and implementation of the Pension Payment Orders.

(a) **PPO Pokhara:** PPO Pokhara is situated in Kaski District of the Western Development Region of Nepal. It started as a seasonal pension paying camp in 1955 and was later established as a permanent PPO in October 1960. PPO Pokhara is responsible for pension disbursement for ESM from Pokhara, Syangja, Gorkha, Tanahun, Lamjung, Palpa and Baglung districts.[111]

(b) **PPO Dharan:** PPO Dharan is located in the eastern region of Nepal. Initially, a seasonal pension paying camp was set up at Dhankuta in 1959 which was later shifted to Dharan as a permanent PPO in 1968. The PPO Dharan is responsible for pension disbursement for ESM from Dharan, Okhaldunga, Diktel, Bhojpur, Tehrathum, Ilam, and Taplejung.

Procedure for Pension Disbursement

Pension Payment Orders/Authorities for payment of pension and other retirement benefits/dues are received by the MPB from respective pension sanctioning authorities, namely, the Principal Controller of Defence Accounts [PCDA(P)], Allahabad, in respect of defence pensioners and from Central Pension Accounting Officer (CPAO), New Delhi, in respect of para-military forces/civilian pensioners of the Central Government. Similarly, pension payment orders/authorities in respect of State Government pensioners are received through the Chief Controller of Accounts, Ministry of External Affairs, New Delhi. Pensioners in Nepal are paid on a monthly basis through banks, once every three months from PPOs and once in six months through Seasonal Pension Paying Camps (SPPCs).[112]

Automation of Pension Payments in Nepal

The pension payment system in Nepal was computerized in 2004 with locally designed pension software that is based on the Oracle platform. The software is in use at all the three PPOs, and had greatly reduced the overall payment time for pensioners; however, the same needs updating. Identification of pensioners – a key requirement for pension payment – has been incorporated into the software, and is achieved through digital photographs of pensioners. Fresh projects for improvement of information technology infrastructure have recently been taken up to ensure timely modernization of existing infrastructure. Extensive use of note-counting machines is made at PPOs and at all cash counters.[113]

Pension Payment through Banks

A pilot project was launched in January 2006 to commence pension payment through banks for pensioners in Kathmandu. The scheme is becoming popular and efforts are being made to encourage maximum pensioners at all places to open bank accounts for pension payments. As on date, 29,884 pensioners are drawing pension through banks.[114]

Record Office of the Indian Embassy

The Record Office in the Indian Embassy (ROIE) Kathmandu is unique and the only Record Office located in a foreign country which functions under the Defence Attaché. Prior to 1947, cases of non-effective Nepal Domiciled Gorkha (NDG) soldiers of the British Army in India were dealt with by the British Legation at Kathmandu. After Independence, the service documents of approximately 30,000 non-effective NDG soldiers were handed over to the Chancery of the Indian Embassy Kathmandu and then to the Military Wing in 1955. Considering the colossal work involved, an Army Record Officer was sanctioned in 1959. At present, ROIE is holding and maintaining 89,323 non-effective service documents.[115]

Besides an Assistant Military Attaché (Record) {AMA (R)} under the Defence Attaché, the ROIE has two JCOs and 24 clerks to handle the work. Two clerks each are based at PPO Pokhara and PPO Dharan for ROIE tasks. The main functions of ROIE are as under:

(a) Investigation of family/dual family pension/Extended Family Pension (EFP) claims.

(b) Payment of death and pensioner benefits to next of kin (NOK).

(c) Payment of all post discharge claims, that is, arrears of pay and allowances and Armed Forces Personnel Provident Fund of NDG pensioners.

(d) Payment of Army Group Insurance money.

(e) Revision of all types of pensions.

(f) Attending to all correspondence, appeals and representations concerning pension, gratuity and other matters.

(g) Verification of all documents relating to re-employment and various grants of NDG soldiers.

(h) Verification of Ex-Servicemen Contributory Health Scheme applications in respect of pensioners and their dependents.

(i) Verification of applications for issue of ESM identity cards.

(j) Issue of relationship certificates to the wards of ESM for enrolment purpose and re-verification of the same when asked by enrolling agencies.

(k) Issue of educational entitlement cards to the wards of battle casualties.

(l) Distribution of PPOs to include service pension, family pension, Enhanced Family Pension (EFP), restoration and revisions.

(m) Documentation and publication of Part II orders in respect of pensioners pertaining to their personal grievances.

(n) Preparation of descriptive roll for identification of pensioners in case any discrepancies are noticed by the pension distributing authority (PDA) during distribution of first pension.

The functions of the ROIE, which is the only one of its types in a foreign country, are more varied and complex than those of other non-effective Record Offices located in India. The recommendation of AMA (R) on pension-related matters is taken as the final input for sanctioning various pensions and other pensioner benefits, as applicable to them. Therefore, the onus of responsibility to establish the genuineness of the NOK after having done thorough investigation lies with AMA (R).[116]

Implementation of the Ex-Servicemen Contributory Health Scheme in Nepal

The Ex-Servicemen Contributory Health Scheme (ECHS) is a flagship welfare scheme of the Government of India, launched on 1 April 2003. The scheme aims to provide quality healthcare to ESM and their dependents through a network of ECHS polyclinics, service medical facilities and civil empanelled/government hospitals spread across the country. The scheme has been structured to provide cashless treatment as far as possible, to its beneficiaries. Treatment provided under ECHS is as per the allopathic medical system and is a government-funded scheme. It was extended to Nepal for Nepal Domiciled Gorkha (NDG) Ex-Servicemen (ESM) with effect from 7 February 2012 wherein the Government of India sanctioned upgradation of three existing medical inspection (MI) rooms to the level of ECHS polyclinics and three mobile clinics.[117]

The government also authorized an ECHS branch, functioning under the Defence Attaché, consisting of one Assistant Military Attaché (ECHS) [AMA(E)] and two India-based clerks to monitor all ECHS-related activities in Nepal.

ECHS polyclinics at Kathmandu, Pokhara and Dharan have been operationalised for treatment of NDG ESM (Armed Forces) and their dependents. For providing cashless specialized medical treatment, the following hospitals in Nepal have been empanelled by ECHS Branch:

(a) Manipal Teaching Hospital, Pokhara.
(b) College of Medical Sciences, Bharatpur.
(c) Lumbini Medical College, Palpa.
(d) Nepalgunj Medical College, Nepalgunj.
(e) B.P. Koirala Institute of Health Sciences, Dharan.
(f) Universal College of Medical Sciences, Bhairahawa.
(g) Gandaki Medical College, Pokhara.

The scheme is compulsory for all fresh retirees and their contribution is being deducted from the Pension Paying Orders at the time of retirement. The contribution for the old retirees, which was earlier deposited by means of military receivable order for which our NDG ESM had to go to India, can now be deposited within Nepal through bank drafts.[118]

NOTES

1. Kirkpatrick, Colonel (1811). *An Account of the Kingdom of Nepaul,* London: William Miller. p. 159. Retrieved 9 March 2012, pp. 55-57.
2. Ibid.
3. Ibid, pp. 162–63.

4. Ibid.
5. Ibid.
6. Ibid.
7. Mahesh C. Regmi. *Kings and Political Leaders of The Gorkhali Empire 1768-1814*, Orient Longman Limited, 1995.
8. Ibid.
9. Francis (Buchanan) Hamilton. *An Account of the Kingdom of Nepal* (reprint of 1819 edn.), New Delhi: Manjusri Publishing House, p. 245.
10. Ibid.
11. History of Nainital District, The Imperial Gazetteer of India 1909, v. 18, pp. 324-325.
12. Ibid.
13. *Historical Dictionary of the British Empire*: A-J, vol. 1; vol. 6, p. 493.
14. Ibid.
15. Ibid.
16. History of Nainital District, The Imperial Gazetteer of India 1909, v. 18, pp. 324-325.
17. History of Nainital District The Imperial Gazetteer of India 1909, v. 18, p. 324-325
18. Ibid.
19. Gerald Bryant (1978). Officers of the East India Company's army in the days of Clive and Hastings, *The Journal of Imperial and Commonwealth History*, 6 (3): 203–27.
20. Gerald Bryant (1978). Officers of the East India Company's army in the days of Clive and Hastings. *The Journal of Imperial and Commonwealth History*, 6 (3): 203–27.
21. Gerald Bryant (1978). Officers of the East India Company's army in the days of Clive and Hastings, *The Journal of Imperial and Commonwealth History*, 6 (3): 203–27.
22. Pemble. *Forgetting and remembering Britain's Gurkha War*, p. 366.
23. Ibid.
24. Ibid.
25. Pemble. *Forgetting and remembering Britain's Gurkha War*, p. 366.
26. Pemble. *Forgetting and remembering Britain's Gurkha War*, p. 366.
27. Ibid.
28. Pemble. *Forgetting and remembering Britain's Gurkha War*, p. 422.
29. Ibid., p. 445.
30. Ibid., p. 467.
31. Pemble. *Forgetting and remembering Britain's Gurkha War*, p. 502.
32. Ibid.
33. Ibid.
34. Ibid.
35. While India sleeps, Chinese threat grows, *Rediff.com News*, 26 May 2008 at http://www.rediff.com/news/column/guest/20080526.htm accessed on 12 April 2016.
36. Fr. Giuseppe. *An Account of Kingdom of Nepal*, vols. I & II; David Reed (2002). *The Rough Guide to Nepal* (third edition), Harrap Colombus, (1799), pp. 307-322.
37. Grover, V. *Nepal: Government and Politics*, Deep & Deep Publications, New Delhi, 2000.
38. Ibid.
39. Thapliyal, S. *Mutual Security: The case of India-Nepal*, Lancer Publishers, New Delhi, 1998, p. 77.
40. Ibid.
41. Bhasin, A.S. (ed.), *Nepal's relations with India and China: documents 1947-1992*, Siba Exim, New Delhi, 1997, p. 83.

42. Authors presence as Defence Attaché in the Indian Embassy in Nepal between 2004 and 2007.
43. Ibid.
44. Ibid.
45. Ibid.
46. Lt-General S.K. Sinha. *Infantry Journal,* 1965.
47. Ibid.
48. Ibid.
49. Ibid.
50. Ibid.
51. Ibid.
52. Ibid.
53. Authors presence as the Defence Attaché in the Indian Embassy in Nepal between 2004 and 2007.
54. Ibid.
55. Ibid.
56. Ibid.
57. Ibid.
58. Ibid.
59. Authors personal knowledge while serving in the Indian army.
60. Nepal's Election and Beyond Crisis Group Asia Report, no. 149, 2 April 2008 at http:/ /www. crisisgroup.org/-/media/Files/asia/south-asia/nepal/149_nepal_s_election_ and_ beyond.ashx accessed on 12 April 2016.
61. Authors presence as the Defence Attaché in the Indian Embassy in Nepal between 2004 and 2007.
62. Ibid.
63. Ibid.
64. Ibid.
65. United Nations Mission in Nepal (UNMIN), The United Nations and Nepal's Peace Process, 2 October 2012.
66. Authors presence as the Defence Attaché in the Indian Embassy in Nepal between 2004 and 2007.
67. Ibid.
68. Ibid.
69. Ibid.
70. Authors presence as the Defence Attaché in the Indian Embassy in Nepal between 2004 and 2007.
71. Jha, P. One country two armies situation ends in Nepal, *The Hindu,* 2 October 2012 at http://www.thehindu.com/news/international/%E2%80%98One-country-two-armies%E2%80%99-situation-ends-in-Nepal/article12542632.ece accessed on 12 March 2015.
72. Ibid.
73. Ibid.
74. Ibid.
75. Jha, P. One country two armies situation ends in Nepal, *The Hindu,* 2 October 2012 at http://www.thehindu.com/news/international/%E2%80%98One-country-two-

armies%E2%80%99-situation-ends-in-Nepal/article12542632.ece accessed on 30 July 2013.

76. Bohara, R. War-makers to peace-keepers, *Nepali Times,* issue 774, September 2015 at http://nepalitimes.com/article/nation/Nepal-from-war-makers-to-peace-keepers,2565 accessed on 12 April 2016.
77. *The Gurkha Soldier,* by Major H.R.K. Gibbs (6th Gurkha Rifles) Deputy Recruiting Officer For Gurkhas, Second edn., Calcutta: Thacker, Spink & Co. (1933) Ltd., I947.
78. Ibid.
79. Ibid.
80. *The Gurkha Soldier,* by Major H.R.K. Gibbs (6th Gurkha Rifles), Deputy Recruiting Officer For Gurkhas, Second edn., Calcutta: Thacker, Spink & Co. (1933) Ltd., I947.
81. Ibid.
82. Ibid.
83. *The Gurkha Soldier,* by Major H.R.K. Gibbs (6th Gurkha Rifles), Deputy Recruiting Officer For Gurkhas, Second edn., Calcutta: Thacker, Spink & Co. (1933) Ltd., I947.
84. Ibid.
85. *The Gurkha Soldier,* by Major H.R.K. Gibbs (6th Gurkha Rifles) Deputy Recruiting Officer For Gurkhas, Second edn. Calcutta: Thacker, Spink & Co. (1933) Ltd., I947.

86 Ibid

87. The Gurkha Soldier, By Major H. R. *K. Gibbs (6th Gurkha Rifles) Deputy Recruiting Officer for Gurkhas, Second Edition* Calcutta Thacker, Spink &Co. (1933) Ltd. I947
88. *The Gurkha Soldier,* by Major H.R.K. Gibbs (6th Gurkha Rifles), Deputy Recruiting Officer For Gurkhas, Second edn., Calcutta: Thacker, Spink & Co. (1933) Ltd., I947.
89. Ibid.
90. Bohara, R. War-makers to peace-keepers, *Nepali Times,* issue 774, September 2015 at http://nepalitimes.com/article/nation/Nepal-from-war-makers-to-peace-keepers,2565 accessed on 12 April 2016.
91. Ibid.
92. Ibid.
93. Ibid.
94. Ibid.
95. Authors experience as the Defence Attaché in the Indian Embassy in Nepal.
96. Ibid.
97. Ibid.

98 Ibid.

99 Ibid.

100 Ibid.

101. Ibid.
102. Ibid.
103. Ibid.
104. Ibid.
105. Ibid.
106. Ibid.
107. Ibid.
108. Ibid.
109. Ibid.

110. Ibid.
111. Ibid.
112. Ibid.
113. Ibid.
114. Ibid.
115. Ibid.
116. Ibid.
117. Ibid.
118. Ibid.

4

Sino-Nepalese Relations and Their Impact on Indo-Nepalese Relations

Historical Perspective

Nepal's relationship with China as the first recorded official engagement dates back to the middle of the seventh century when Nepal's armed forays into Tibet led to Chinese intervention in favour of the latter. It resulted in the signing of the Sino-Nepalese Treaty of 1792, which provided for a tribute-bearing mission from Nepal to China every five years as a symbol of China's political and economic supremacy in the region.[1]

Tibet has been the focal point in their off-and-on relations for many years till 1814-16 when British India entered as another important contender for Nepali loyalties. It was during the first Anglo-Nepalese war of 1814 when China refused to come to Nepal's aid and voluntarily ceded its dominant position in Nepal to the growing British influence in the region. In 1856, the Treaty of Thapathali was signed between China and Nepal, after Nepal invaded Tibet which forced Nepal to accept China's special status as well as made it obligatory for Kathmandu to come to Tibet's rescue in case of any foreign invasion.[2]

However, Nepal refused to honour its obligation to Tibet when the colonial power of the British-Indian army invaded Tibet in 1910. This created shock waves in China about Britain's designs. Later, in 1911, Nepal reneged from its treaty with China and declared that it would help Tibet attain independent status if it suited British interests.[3] This break between Kathmandu and Beijing lasted till 1955, when relations were re-established with China. Subsequently, a treaty of peace and friendship was signed between them in 1960.[4]

Tracing back to India's independence in 1947, followed by the founding of the People's Republic of China (PRC) in 1949, which announced the liberation of Tibet as an immediate goal, New Delhi turned its gaze towards the security of its northern borders.[5] Prime Minister Jawaharlal Nehru on the issue of the border was influenced by two strands of thought.

After the 29 April 1954 signing of the India-China Agreement on Trade and Intercourse between Tibet Region of China and India in which India for the first time accepted Tibet as a part of China, Nehru and his associates thought that the boundary was no longer an issue and that the Chinese accepted the historical status quo. Second, friendship with China was of over-riding importance; the border issue was less important and the status of Tibet expendable.[6] This search for Sino-Indian friendship, whether out of a common anti-imperialist agenda or Asian solidarity, pervaded all aspects of Indian policy towards China, exhibiting a mind-boggling degree of naiveté or a rare act of selflessness in international politics.[7]

The 1962 border war with China changed India's practice, if not its policy, towards the Tibetan refugees. Then Prime Minister Rajiv Gandhi's visit to Beijing in 1989 brought about temporary relief or a thaw in relations and a return to India's pre-1962 policy statement on Tibet, although there have been no discernible practical fall-outs on the Tibetan exiles.

Maintaining a balancing relationship with China is one of the key and critical components of Nepal's China policy. At the other end of the spectrum, there is always one or the other country which Nepal considers crucial for its own survival given its delicate landlocked position between India and China, the two emerging Asian superpowers. Earlier, it was Britain whose overwhelming presence in South Asia, and India in particular, gave enough reason for Nepal to sometimes take an independent look at its relationship with China. It was Britain which soon after the Anglo-Nepalese War in 1816 made Nepal sign the Treaty of Sugauli, which settled Nepal's present-day boundaries by quashing its claims over the disputed Terai (low lands) territories.[8]

Later, post the retreat of Britain in 1947, the vacuum that was created in the power equation was sought to be filled by India which tried to emerge as one of the more formidable powers in South Asia. This initial thrust starting from 1950 resulted in the initiation of two important treaties; firstly, the Indo-Nepal Treaty of Peace and Friendship, and secondly, the Trade and Transit Treaty. These treaties provided the basis for the initiation of emerging bilateral relations between a newly independent India and Nepal.[9]

However, this led to identification of many similarities and mutual complementarities which, although well-intended, resulted in the creation of suspicion in the minds of the Nepalese politicians about newly independent India and her intentions. They also felt that these treaties continuously reminded them of their own perceptions of their inferior status vis-à-vis India.

Later in the seventies, there was a series of events which included the Indo-Soviet Treaty of Peace, Friendship and Cooperation in 1971, the Indo-Pak War and the creation of Bangladesh, the merger of Sikkim in India in 1974 and later, India's unofficial support to the political opposition in Nepal. Further, along the Indo-Nepal border, there was the alarming rise of Naxalism in the areas of Siliguri and Naxalbari in West Bengal which created a great deal of apprehension in the minds of the King of Nepal and his coterie of advisors who felt that the spillover of this movement could result in a greater problem in Nepal, especially given the wide disparity in the living standards of the people of Nepal.[10] Later, India's nuclear explosion in 1974 and her decision to emerge as a nuclear power added to Nepal's discomfiture and fuelled her insecurity about the impact of India's growing stature as a regional power and her intentions towards Nepal.[11]

The border dispute between India and China over Tibet continues to remain a matter of conflict, despite six decades of resolution. Both New Delhi and Beijing have used the Tibet issue only to regulate their broader bilateral relations, including on the border issue, rather than actively pushing for the resolution of the Sino-Tibetan conflict.[12]

It is in this context that Nepal restarted and reshaped its ties with China as a possible counterweight to India. Certain international events too influenced this decision of going back to China, most important was the sudden loss of India in the Indo-China border war in 1962 and the beginning of aggressive Chinese posturing with regard to the continual disputed border claims with India.[13] This caused a great deal of alarm in the Nepali power and political structures that felt that China, if not influenced now, would do the same to them sooner rather than later. Further, this insecurity of Nepal also propelled China to start thinking of the consolidation of her presence within Nepal, discerning correctly that it would be fairly easy to prop up the Nepali power structure against India if and when the need arose given Nepal's insecurity and apprehensions.[14]

Since then, both the countries are seen as vying with each other to influence the Nepali polity to their satisfaction. Tibet remains a key irritant in India-China relations. To support these claims about the geo-strategic rivalry between China and India, the following issues are the main issues – the status of Tibet, Chinese unease with the activities of Tibetan refugees, including the Dalai Lama, Indian fears over Chinese military presence on the Tibetan plateau and the long-standing border dispute.[15]

Nepal is clearly aware that it is impossible for it to cut off its relations with India especially since they are so deeply intertwined with each other into what they call the *Roti-Beti* relationship.[16]

Nepal's relationship with China is need-based and practical; it lacks the warmth and depth of India-Nepal relations, no matter how flawed it probably is. It is evident from the past that both China and Nepal are prone to ditching each other whenever the circumstances change and the power situation demands. On the other hand, India and Nepal share a deep and enduring relationship cemented by shared history and culture, irrespective of posturing by the current political leadership, and visits by Nepali political leaders to China and vice versa.

China's main interest in Nepal has always been led by its concerns over Tibet, which has been ruled by China since 1950. Beijing's involvement with Nepal grew much more intense after the March 2008 ethnic Tibetan uprising against Chinese rule, which deeply embarrassed the Chinese government on the eve of its 2008 Olympic Games. There are an estimated 25,000 Tibetans living in Nepal but with China pushing Nepal to tighten its border with Tibet, the number of new refugees reaching Nepal has dropped to a trickle from an earlier annual figure of around 2,500. It too has increased its focus on economic ties; trade between China and Nepal has quadrupled since 2003.[17]

Unified in the 18th century by King Prithvi Narayan Shah of Gorkha with a majority of its Hindu population and with deep historical and cultural relations with India, Nepal had been governed by a prime minister, a member of the Rana family who were allies of the British, with the title of Maharaja, a few years post Nepal's defeat in the war with the British (1814-1816). The Treaty of Sugauli signed on 2 December 1815 had preserved the independence of the Nepali kingdom at the cost of large territorial concessions to the East India Company.[18]

While the Chinese, during the last period of the Manchu dynasty, were invading Tibet, it was very important for the British Government who also wrote to the Government of India to clarify the nature of the relations of the Kingdom of Nepal with China. The English, of course, could not accept any claim of China over Nepal. The Chinese used to address the King of Nepal with the title of Wang.[19] It seemed that China was using that title for the Nepalese monarch with the idea of addressing a vassal of the Chinese Empire. The first treaty between Nepal and Tibet dates back to 1789 when Tibet, defeated by Nepal, had pledged to pay an annual tribute to Nepal. After that, in the following year, the Ching Emperor Chien-lung sent to Rana Bahadur Shah, the King of Nepal, in response to the first tribute sent from Nepal to China, a patent in which Rana Bahadur

Shah was inserted among the tributaries of the Empire, conferring on him the title of Ertini Wang (Prince of the Law).

In 1791, Nepal invaded Tibet again but this resulted in a victory of the Ching over Nepal in 1792, a victory that forced Nepal to pay a quinquennial tribute to China.[20]

The Nepalese had sent missions with gifts to the Manchu Emperor every five years (although that term time had not always been respected), but this tribute was regarded in a different way and stated that this tribute was a simple exchange of gifts between two independent countries. The Prime Minister of Nepal, Chandra Shumsher Jung Bahadur Rana (1863-1929), tried to clarify this issue in his letters to the British Resident in Nepal, Lieutenant Colonel John Manners Smith:

> "Our relations with China though of long standing have always been regarded by us as that of a simple, friendly, and innocent nature. The missions that proceed from this country to China were of the nature of embassies from one court to another, which were invariably treated with honour and consideration due to honoured foreign guests and their expenses were entirely borne by the Chinese government...."[21]

Further, Nepal did not just declare the total independence of the country from China, but also claimed full independence of Nepal from the United Kingdom which had in addition to not recognizing the representative of Nepal as an ambassador, had also put Nepal in a list among the many Native States that were under the colonial power in India. In another letter of 1906, Chandra Shumsher further clarified the exclusive commercial nature of the quinquennial mission: "I may here add that the practice of sending a mission was inaugurated soon after the war between this country and China in 1792 and this practice has since been kept up for its commercial advantages more than for anything else.[22] The few presents which the mission carried to China were not of much value and certainly not like a tribute. The customary letter which is sent on the occasion was written in the truly oriental style of exuberant but meaningless politeness and follows a stereotyped rule. They are merely a means for the party to gain access into the country under very advantageous circumstances and to dispose with very great profit the large number of goods which they take with them. It may be known to you that all gifts were carried free from our frontier to Peking and back by transport provided by the Chinese government which also freely provided our men with all the necessaries on the road. These gifts had very little political significance. Moreover, our relations and the trade and other facilities which we enjoy in Tibet make it incumbent upon us to keep this harmless and friendly practice as this country has a very considerable interest as well as various rights and privileges in the said country, commercial and otherwise."[23]

Further the Nepali Maharaja went on to add, "It will be seen that Nepal alone retains any remains of independence, and, standing isolated, encompassed by our territories, that state has, as regards external politics, as little independent action as any other. But in its internal affairs we have never attempted to interfere. The Resident is rather an ambassador than a supervisor. Nepal, therefore, might be formidable if it had the means, but our security is in the smallness of its revenue. Its territory is almost entirely mountain, yields a comparatively small sum, and its army is very small. It is formidable on the defensive, but would be contemptible on the offensive."

In response, Lieutenant Colonel Manners Smith explained to the Nepalese Prime Minister that although they cannot lawfully grant the title of Ambassador to the representative of the King of Nepal, that did not mean a change in the accorded treatment. Further, Manners Smith justified the last edition of the *Imperial Gazetteer* as an attempt to explain the relations between India and Nepal, ensuring the Nepalese Durbar that there was no offensive intention or aimed to diminish the status and privileges of the Durbar.[24] The Maharaja showed to Manners Smith the original letter, dated 31 March 1885, written by Lord Dufferin, Governor General and Viceroy of India (1884-1888) to the Nepalese Prime Minister of the time, Ranodip Singh Kunwar, in which the then Viceroy of India defined the Himalayan country as an independent state.

In 1893, Viceroy of India Lord Lansdowne informed the Nepalese Durbar of the British approval to sell and import weapons to Nepal, in reasonable quantities, but during the following years there have been differences of opinion between the Durbar and the Government of India as to what may be considered the reasonable requirements of the status of Nepal. The Government of India had consistently refused to allow the Durbar to import machinery for the manufacture of warlike stores. Manners Smith, for conciliating the Durbar, proposed to the Government of India that the Durbar should now be informed that they were at liberty to import such machinery and stores and to provide to the Nepalese army magazine rifles, in order that they might be available for Imperial defence when required. Subsequently, a letter from then Nepalese Prime Minister, Chandra Shumsher, to Manners Smith, dated 19 November 1910, stated that: "At the same time Nepal stands apart from the Indian protectorate, and is very jealous of any interference. It has in times past settled its own quarrels with Tibet, and is entitled to have its own Resident at Lhasa. Its army is efficient, and would probably give effect to any policy in Tibet which the Prime Minister might decide upon. In view of the considerations, it is of the utmost importance to avoid a collision between Nepal and its neighbours."[25]

The Government of India further informed that London would continue to protect Nepal in case of unprovoked attack and that so long as the prime minister consults the British Government and follows their advice when given, and preserves his present and friendly attitude, His Majesty's Government will not allow the interests and rights of Nepal to be affected or prejudiced by any administrative changes in Tibet. A position to which the Government of India, the India Office, the Foreign Office, and the rest of the UK government agreed. In June 1911, instead of the machinery, the Government of India proposed to the India Office (which agreed) to donate, on the occasion of the visit of the King of Nepal, 2,000 Lee-Metford rifles together with 500,000 cartridges.[26] Thus, on 1 May 1911, it was Manners Smith's duty to reassure the Nepalese Prime Minister, announcing: "The positions of the Raj and also that the Government of India are glad to meet your Excellency's wishes in the matter, and I am to say, therefore, that the Government of India have no desire whatever to interfere with the independent position which the State of Nepal has hitherto enjoyed. The British would continue to support Nepal, while the Himalayan kingdom would continue to send Gorkha soldiers in the hour of need."[27]

Tibet and Nepal have had relations since recorded history began. In his book, *Tibet, a History*, Sam Van Schaik, has spoken of this relationship as early as 700 CE where he states, "In the early days of the Tibetan empire, Tibetans were influenced by cultures as far afield as Persia, Nepal, and Korea."[28] Tibet has long been a market place for merchants and pilgrims travelling from nearby Asian countries for trade. In fact, Tibet's history is not one of the erstwhile thought mythical isolations, but of a thriving civilisation and a marketplace. Further, he goes on to say, "The pressure of the Indian subcontinent has pushed up some of the highest mountains in the world to wall the Tibetan plateau.[29] The geographical location of Tibet is south-west of China, bordering India, Nepal, Burma, and Bhutan. To the west are located the Karakoram Mountains and to the north, are the Kunlun Mountain ranges; further to the south and to the east are the Himalayas. Across the Himalayas, the Kingdom of Nepal has always existed and the prosperous Kathmandu valley, which was in many ways a trading post which benefitted a vast number of traders who passed through the Kingdom of Nepal to either India in the south of China and Tibet in the north."[30]

The relations between Nepal and China date back to the middle of the fifth century BCE. Traders, scholars, soldiers, philosophers, artists, traders, and adventurers travelled exchanging news, gifts, inventions, and commercial opportunities. In fact, it was a Nepali architect, Arniko, who is supposed to have created and supervised the construction of the White Pagoda in 1278 during the Yuan Dynasty. This pagoda created by Arniko in Beijing, which still stands today, has become a standard of architecture in China, Korea and Japan. The highway that connects Kathmandu with the Tibetan border and continues on to Lhasa is called the Arniko Highway in memory of this great architect. The road runs first along the Sun Kosi or Golden River, then the Bhote Kosi or Tibet River. It was built with China's assistance in the 1960s, after the Sino-Indian war.

Many Chinese philosophers and learned Buddhist monks travelled the Silk Route seeking intellectual and spiritual exchanges with scholars along the Ganges (now Ganga) plains to South India and Sri Lanka. Chinese scholar and traveller Hiuen Tsang (603-664 CE), in particular, left records about his visit to Nepal.[31]

Nepal's China Relationship (18th-20th Centuries)

The 18th century saw the advent of the modern state of Nepal with the unifier, King Prithvi Narayan Shah and his successors expanding its territory towards the west, north and the south which included forays into Tibet. The Chinese intervened in favour of Tibet and defeated the Nepali armies, thereby forcing Nepal into signing the Chinese-Nepali Treaty of Betrawati in 1792 that ensured tribute-paying missions to the Emperor of the Chinese Kingdom every five years (till 1908). This treaty became symbolic of the Chinese political and cultural supremacy over Tibet. Later, during the Anglo-Nepali war of 1834, when the King of Nepal asked the Chinese Emperor for military assistance against the British East India's armies, he was refused. Keeping in mind the superiority of the British colonial army, the Chinese Emperor effectively surrendered control over both Tibet and Nepal to the expanding British colonial power.

Later, when Nepal again invaded Tibet in 1854, China once again intervened militarily and forced the Kingdom of Nepal to sign the Treaty of Thapathali in March 1856. This treaty explicitly recognised China's influence over Tibet and further forced Nepal to give a yearly tribute (until 1953) to China and committed Nepal to assist Tibet in the event of any foreign aggression. However, towards the end of the 19th century, Nepal aligned itself with the British Raj in India, contributing immensely to the colonial armies that fought in both the world wars as well as assisted the British to suppress the innumerable small rebellions that were emanating in India and later also assisted their military expeditionary force into Tibet. In 1904, the British army marched to Lhasa in order to prevent Russia extending its influence into Tibet. This time Nepal rejected Tibet's request for assistance.

The Anglo-Chinese Convention of 1906 had recognized Chinese sovereignty over the region. However, when China sought to claim Tibet in 1910, Nepal sided with Tibet and Britain. Nepal then broke relations with China after Tibet drove the Chinese forces out in 1911 in the wake of the Chinese Revolution (the Xinhai Revolution of 1911 which led Emperor Puyi to abdicate). China then concentrated on its revolutions, civil wars, invasions, famines, the Second World War spreading into its territory and the ultimate creation of the Communist People's Republic. Until 1949, Tibet remained independent from all such events and their influence.[32]

Nepal's China Policy in the Second Half of the 20th Century

Nepal's China policy is best understood in relation to events linked with India: two years after the end of the Second World War, India gained its independence and the British Raj left the subcontinent. The separation of its Muslim population into a two-part Pakistan (East and West) occurred in an atmosphere of mistrust that turned into hatred. The migration of the settled population between Pakistan and India was undertaken with great brutality. Three wars between them and countless skirmishes, particularly in the northwest (Kashmir), have kept India in a heightened state of conflict in the region for over 60 years. As explained, independent India was surrounded by real or potential foes and therefore, the security of India depended on its ability to outwardly and inwardly manage its neighbours. In the early 1950s, Indian military missions included the provision of training for Nepali troops and the posting of Indian military personnel along the northern border (in 1951, also in response to China annexing Tibet. This military mission withdrew on the request of Nepal in 1969).[33]

China's Foreign Policy Aims in Nepal

The strategic location of Nepal between India and China lends itself to the fact that the slightest stir in Nepal will have a residual effect on both India and China, especially Tibet. Apart from the economic and trade interest of both the countries, they also have interest in containing US influences in the region. Both countries consider the other as competitors and there is considerable trust deficit between them post the 1962 war.

Tibet became strategically important for both China and Nepal since both wanted to keep Nepal within their respective spheres of influence. From the south, Nepal is the gateway to the Tibet Autonomous Region (TAR), which plays an important role in China's South Asia outreach and also is the gateway to the Indo-Gangetic plains of India, in many ways the heartland of India. The Tibet issue, which is China's great security concern, has become a major determinant of Chinese foreign policy towards Nepal, specifically to reiterate a historical fact that the Khampa rebels of Tibet used Nepal's territory in 1959. Nepal on the other hand has over the last century remained within India's security system.[34]

China remains sensitive to Nepal being used by external powers to challenge its strategic interests in Tibet especially by the USA in its larger strategy of encircling China.[35] During the 1960s, there were several demonstrations in Kathmandu as well as in Tibet by Tibetan expatriates who had their homes in Nepal. This led China to be suspicious of this external engagement of Nepal as it was concerned with foreign forces that were engaged in instigating anti-China activities in Nepal and Tibet.

Prior to 1950, when Tibet was not a part of China, Nepal had closer relations with Tibet. After Tibet became a part of China, Nepal established diplomatic relations with China in 1955. A close scrutiny of Nepal-China relations reveals that financial aspects, especially trade, have always regulated the sphere of diplomatic relations between the two countries.

20th Century Engagement

> *Nepal can neither find an alternative to its centuries-old relations with India nor can it isolate itself from China and its prosperity. Nepal's only aim is to extract the maximum benefit from both the neighbours. Neither of our neighbours should be suspicious of our relations with them.*
>
> – Foreign Minister of Nepal Pradeep Kumar Gyawali.

Chinese interests in Nepal are Tibet-centric and her objectives in Nepal are the security of Chinese interests in Tibet. Given the earlier regular flow of Tibetan refugees into Nepal and India every year, China's objective is to nullify any negative fallout.

The prime motive of China in the first phase (1955 to 1989)[36] was to create infrastructure in Nepal. China also promised Nepal to protect its territory from any third country. China openly exhorted Nepali assertions of independence vis-à-vis India throughout the period up to 1978. Intense anti-Indian propaganda was directed by China into Nepal.[37]

The second phase of Chinese policy focused on ending Nepal's overdependence on India. Till 1995, trade between China and Nepal was limited to 0.7 per cent. The remaining 99.03[38] per cent trade was with India. China was conscious of the geographical proximity between India and Nepal. Therefore, new routes to trade in Nepal were planned. China encouraged Nepal to adopt the equidistance policy between India and China. In the early years, Chinese assistance was pledged in terms of projects and a number of financial involvements were initiated. From the mid-90s, the Chinese government has been pledging to grant assistance to Nepal under the economic and technical cooperation programme in order to implement mutually acceptable development projects. The volume of such assistance had been averaging 80 million yuan every year.

21st Century Engagement

There is now little doubt that India has lost strategic space to China in Nepal. Some reckon the era of special relations between India and Nepal is nearly over as China makes steady inroads. There has been a truly breathtaking rise in Chinese influence and a corresponding fall in Indian sway in Nepal. The 2015-16 India-inspired blockade of the India-Nepal border imposed, in part, owing to India's displeasure over the new constitution Nepal had just promulgated seems to have been the catalyst.

At US$ 79.26 million, China accounts for nearly 60 per cent of foreign direct investment (FDI) commitments received by Nepal in the first half of the current fiscal year beginning mid-July 2017. India is a distant second with US$ 36.63 million, followed by the USA and Japan. As China closes in, it severely restricts the clout India once enjoyed in the peripheral countries of her neighbourhood. However, of all the peripheral countries, the geostrategic location of Nepal gives it particular importance since it is at the head of the critical Indo-Gangetic plains, India's heartland, and provides a critical buffer with China.

In this third and most aggressive phase, China has adopted a posture to weaken India's hold on Nepal. This phase continued the agenda of the first and second phases but the focus increased more towards encircling India. Towards this, it is apparent that China is not only courting the Nepalese Maoists, but also rendering political as well material support to the Indian Maoists whose ultimate aim is to overthrow the parliamentary democracy through an armed struggle. The sheer political capital of the Maoists, and the anti-China protests of March 2008 in various parts of Tibet including Sichuan, underscored the importance of Nepal for China, mainly because Nepal gives sanctuary to close to 20,000 expatriate Tibetan community.[39]

Nepal has become the latest proxy battleground between the regional powers, India and China, to demonstrate their influence. New Delhi is increasingly getting worried about China's creeping influence in Nepal as China has managed to project itself as a disinterested neighbour and a remarkably attractive alternative to Big Brother India.[40] However, even as Nepal's Prime Minister Prachanda spoke of the need to review the Indo-Nepal Friendship Treaty of 1950 which Nepal accepted, a draft of a Peace and Friendship Treaty was submitted by China.

Human Resource

China has established a number of China study centres (CSC) in Nepal. These provide Chinese language and culture classes and are manned by volunteers from China which assist it in educating the common Nepali about information about Chinese social and economic development in Nepal as well as provide them with a convenient platform for the dissemination of Chinese policy towards South Asia and India's role therein.[41]

The Confucius Institute at Kathmandu University which celebrated its sixth anniversary in June 2013, with an aim to provide training to students and teachers, runs numerous programmes from business management to tour guide training across Nepal. Now, Nepali students even those with just primary school education have access to Chinese language lessons and exposure to Chinese culture. Apart from these, numerous local level organisations have been established including the Nepal-China Youth Friendship Association and the Nepal-China Mutual Cooperation Society to foster cooperation at all levels.[42]

Trade and Investment

> *We have great connectivity with India and an open border. All that's fine and well increase connectivity even further, but we can't forget that we have two neighbours. We don't want to depend on one country or have one option.*
>
> —K.P. Sharma Oli, former Prime Minister of Nepal

The Himalayas were the arena where British India and China competed for influence earlier, because of the *Old Great game*. The *ring fence* system operated by Britain resulted in an independent but friendly and cooperative Nepal, with Sikkim and Bhutan as Indian protectorates, and with Tibet as an autonomous buffer state, guaranteeing India's commercial and strategic interests. One hundred years later, similar dynamics and similar concerns were in play for India. Prime Minister Jawaharlal Nehru, the chief architect of India's foreign policy, wanted to continue the British policy towards the Himalayan states but was unable to do so. This might have been due to lack of a long-term strategic vision or the excessively idealistic structures of Indian foreign policy. The fault lines in the Indian policy on Tibet became apparent after 1951. Post-independence, India followed the policy laid down by the British and treated Tibet as an autonomous buffer state between India and China, accepting the concept of a vague Chinese suzerainty but not sovereignty over Tibet. Thus, in March 1947, a Tibetan delegation was invited to the Asian Relation's Conference in Delhi, despite protests from Chinese (Kuomintang) delegates.

Nehru wanted to protect India's security interests in the Himalayan regions. As the Chinese communists neared their revolutionary victory, Nehru rushed through a series of defence treaties with Bhutan (August 1949), Nepal (July 1950) and Sikkim (December 1950). These countries constituted Nehru's redrawn security zone.

In February 1951, he established the North and North-Eastern Defence Committee and visited the North-East Frontier Agency (NEFA), Sikkim, and Bhutan. China's long-term game plan in Nepal and its security and foreign policy objectives in Nepal are several. Nepal and China share a long border, spanning about 1,414 kilometres. China has been playing a significant role in determining the future shape of Nepali politics. The continuous political victories of one form or the other of the Communist Party of Nepal seems to have spurred China to adopt its engagement with Nepal on the basis of a long-term plan which seems to be enabling Chinese involvement in everyday life in a manner which is seemingly benign but very much capable of shaping attitudes towards China and India in the years to come.

In May 1994, Nepal and China signed an auto transport agreement on the Lhasa-Kathmandu route. In 1999, they signed the notes of agreement on cross-border grazing. In July 2002, they signed an agreement on trade and other issues between Tibet Autonomous Region of China and Nepal.[43]

The Chinese interest lies in investing in hotels, restaurants, electronics, cell phone services, radio paging services, readymade garments, nursing homes, hydropower, civil construction, and the like. By mid-2013, there were 25 industries operating under Chinese investment while six more were under construction and 13 more were licensed.[44]

On the issue of connectivity, K.P. Sharma Oli, the then Prime Minister of Nepal, articulated clearly that once China brings its rail network up to Shigatse and then Kyirong in Tibet, it should be easy to extend it to Nepal. Its altitude is lower than Tibet, and the terrain actually slopes all the way down from Kyirong. Apart from that, three roads are under construction connecting China and Nepal, which should be ready in a couple of years. If we can connect this railway network to our east-west rail project, it can revolutionise China-India trade, with Nepal in the middle.

The construction of a road link between Lhasa and Khasa, a border town located 80 kilometres north of Kathmandu, is functional. Furthermore, China has also accepted Nepal's proposal to open up two more customs points in addition to the existing five. China is also building a 65 kilometre second road link, the Syabrubesi-Rasuwagadhi road, which is the shortest route from Tibet to Kathmandu. As part of promoting Nepal's hydro-power projects, in 2008, China's Assistant Minister for Foreign Affairs, He Yafei, pledged to provide Nepal a loan of US$ 125 million for the hydropower projects Upper Trishuli 3A and US$ 62 million for Upper Trishuli 3B.[45]

In August 2008, China handed over to Nepal a new information superhighway between China and Nepal, a 100 kilometre Zhangmu-Kathmandu optical fibre cable project. Moreover, Chinese contractors are also involved in the construction of the Melamchi water supply project in Central Nepal to alleviate the perpetual water shortage in the capital. The first phase of this three-phase project, budgeted at US$ 317.3 million was completed by end 2013. The government of Nepal has invited Chinese support and participation in the development of Nepal's hydroelectric potential and China has already invested almost US$ 200 million in various such projects.

In recent years, there has been a gradual shift in China's focus from the eastern seaboard to south-west China such as Tibet, Quighai, Gunsu, Sichuan, Kunming, and Xinjiang, which are in the immediate neighbourhood of Nepal. Nepal is assuming a new geo-strategic eminence as a buffer zone between India and China, particularly for the defensive build-up in the Tibetan plateau, construction of the Karakoram highway, the rail link from Beijing to Lhasa and now from Lhasa towards Nepal and Sikkim.

The Himalayas have now become the southern border of the People's Republic of China, and they are right in the middle of India's Himalayan frontiers, and are in fact its northern borderland flanks.

There has been a major shift in China's foreign policy towards Nepal since the Maoist ascendance to power. China had earlier adopted a policy of non-intervention in the internal matters of Nepal and largely stayed out of Nepalese internal politics. However, the demise of the monarchy and the ascendance of the Maoists that it had only recently termed as anti-government forces parties, have forced China to quickly reshape its Nepal policy. Consequently, China has sought to engage Nepalese political actors at all levels, primarily to secure the border with Nepal. With the Maoists in power, China also hopes to use its ideological commonalities to suppress the Tibetan movement in Nepal.

When the Maoists emerged victorious in the April 2008 elections, China adopted a wait and watch policy because it was unsure of their intentions as China felt that the Maoists were backed by India and were catapulted to the political centre stage only after a comprehensive peace agreement in which India had played a substantial behind-the-scenes role. However, with their victory in the 2017 elections, media reports reveal that after several interactions with Maoists leaders, China has begun to feel quite comfortable with the Prime Minister Oli-led Maoist government. The Maoists ideological linkages with China and their keenness to neutralise India's influence in the region have also made them an obvious choice for engagement.

It has been reported that in interactions with the Chinese, Maoist leaders gave the impression that the future of democracy in Nepal could be guided by the example of the Communist Party of China. Indeed, there were many in Nepal who argued that persistence with the Maoist tag in the party name despite joining competitive politics indicates that the party may work towards a single party system in the future, given that dictatorship of the proletariat has a prime place in the Maoist lexicon. In fact, some hard line leaders of the party have suggested a people's republic similar to that of China on a number of occasions even after the Maoists joined the political mainstream. These ideas might have encouraged China to attempt to consolidate its position in Nepal by continuously engaging the Maoists at the political, economic, military, and social levels, and thus secure its strategic interests in the region.

The Maoist-led government was also asked by China to adopt a One-China policy, not allow Nepalese land to be used for anti-China activities, take strong action against Tibetan refugees, and grant special facilities for Chinese investments in strategic sectors. Beijing has also initiated Track II diplomacy with Nepal and invited Nepalese scholars to undertake visits to Chinese think tanks. In 2009, Chinese Foreign Minister Yang Jiechi stated in Beijing that China would prefer to work with Nepal on the basis of a strategic partnership.

Considering the strategic and economic interests Beijing has in Nepal, in terms of energy from hydro projects and as a transit country between China and India, China may further expand its state-level engagements by entering into long-term agreements at various levels. The proposed new friendship treaty marks the beginning of this process. Moreover, the treaty may enhance the bargaining power of the Maoist government vis-à-vis India to resolve some of the long-standing disputes between the two countries.

Any foreign presence in Nepal is a concern for India. Given the centuries-old socio-cultural and economic ties between India and Nepal, the Indo-Nepal relationship was acknowledged as unassailable during the official visit of Nepalese Prime Minister Pushpa Kamal Dahal to New Delhi in September 2008 and an equidistance policy can only come at the expense of India-Nepal relations.

The Chinese presence in Nepal and its dubious plans are a real threat. Nepal, being a sovereign country would like to deal with India on an equitable basis. Given geographically contiguous, culturally similar, and economically close relationship with India, Nepal perhaps also realizes that it would be quite impractical to ignore its southern giant at the behest of building strategic ties with the northern giant. With globalisation, shifting Asian balance of power, the rise of China and emergence of India, Nepal is, thus, likely to opt for a balanced approach with both India and China, which it hopes would eventually pave the path for its own economic growth and stability. For India, the challenge is to keep Nepal within its sphere of influence without being seen as domineering. In fact, India has to deftly handle its Nepal policy keeping in mind the growing Chinese presence in Nepal.

China is currently working on the reconstruction of the China-Nepal highway. Built at a cost of over US$ 100 million, there are only two sections of the highway on the Chinese side, the Tingri to Nyalam and Nyalam to Zhangmu sections that are pending completion. Once complete, the highway is expected to become a golden gateway connecting Lhasa to Kathmandu and will be China's gateway to South Asia. Taken along with the Qinghai-Tibet railroad, this highway has been touted as having the potential to boost Nepal's economic growth through greater trade with China.

It is evident that China's engagement with Nepal is a long-term plan which enables the Chinese to plan their involvement so that it is capable of shaping attitudes of the Nepalese towards China positively and towards

India negatively in the years to come. China's biggest strength has been its ability to formulate and execute timely, objective-oriented, action strategies in diplomatic, economic, and military fronts for three decades. China's multifaceted military capability has been demonstrated in recent years in cyber warfare, space missions and anti-satellite warfare, developing and producing fighter aircraft, building an aircraft carrier, and building a modern submarine fleet. India's modest strategic response to these developments had been reactive, lacking long-term vision. While its space, missile, naval, air force and electronic warfare capabilities are progressing, the process appears to lack dynamism and commitment to produce timely results. Due to lack of goal clarity, even the few successful initiatives have not translated into any strategic advantage.

India also does not appear to be taking full advantage of its geo-strategic advantage that it enjoys by virtue of its location between Central and Southeast Asia. Even in South Asia, only during the last decade or so, has she started seriously efforts to build strategic relations with its neighbours like Myanmar, Bangladesh, and Sri Lanka. However, Nepal, with which it has a complex relationship, seems to be an exception, because of various domestic and external considerations.

China's engagement in Nepal offers immense economic packages, diplomatic and security offers, and development projects so as to gain a strategic foothold in Nepal. China's decision to increase ties with Nepal grew much more intense after the March 2008 ethnic Tibetan uprising against Chinese rule, just prior to the 2008 Olympic Games that were held in Beijing. There are an estimated 25,000 Tibetans living in Nepal but, with China pushing Nepal to tighten its border with Tibet, the number of new refugees reaching Nepal has dropped to a trickle from an earlier annual figure of around 2,500. China has increased its focus on economic ties and has quadrupled it since 2003.

Nepali perception of India's South Asian policy, as being hegemonic, and interfering in Nepal's internal affairs is additionally keeping them wary and moving them farther away from India. The economic power of China and its aggressive South Asian policy are also providing room for China to increase its strategic clout within Nepal.

India needs to develop railway and road connectivity with Nepal and needs to give priority to Nepal's hydropower development in light of the fact that it is an also a potential market. Tardy implementation of infrastructure projects has remained an unfortunate feature of India's policy with her neighbours, which had led to growing perception in Nepal that India promises, China delivers. India's record of project implementation in Nepal is extremely poor and in fact in most cases negligible.

Considering the above issues which highlight indulgence of China in Nepal on issues which cover the complete canvas from directing internal politics, trade and commerce, infrastructure development, tourism, construction of strategically important roads and railway lines, is a clear indication of increased Chinese interest in Nepal and the South Asia region which is strategically a cause of concern for India in handling the long-term simmering security threat.

NOTES

1. *Kirkpatrick, Colonel (1811). An Account of the Kingdom of Nepaul. London, William Miller,* retrieved 11 February 2013.
2. Ibid.
3. Ibid.
4. Ibid.
5. Topgyal, Tsering (2011). Charting the Tibet Issue in the Sino"Indian Border Dispute, *China Report,* 47, 2 (2011): 115–131.
6. Garver, 2001: 89–90; Norbu, 2001:
7. Topgyal, 2011; 121.
8. Ibid.
9. Ibid.
10. http://www.telegraphnepal.com/national/2011-07-27/nepal:-king-birendras-zone-of-peace-discussed
11. Ibid.
12. Topgyal 2011:116
13. Ibid.
14. http://www.telegraphnepal.com/national/2011-07-27/nepal:-king-birendras-zone-of-peace-discussed
15. Topgyal 2011:117.
16. Ibid.
17. Tenzin, Acharya Kirti Tulku Lobsang. Early Relations between Tibbet and Nepal (7th to 8th Centuries), Translated by K. Dhondup. *The Tibet Journal,* vol. VII, nos. 1 & 2. Spring/Summer 1982, p. 84.
18. Text of the treaty in C.U. AITCHISON (ed.), A Collection of Treaties, Engagements, and Sunnuds, Relating to India and Neighbouring Countries, vol. 2, Calcutta, 1876, pp.,166-168.

19. On 7 March 1911, Jordan sent to Lord Hardinge, Viceroy of India, the English translations, composed by Edmund Backhouse, of the Manchu patents granted to the king in 1790 and to the Nepalese Prime Minister Jang Bahadur Rana in 1870.
20. Text of the treaty in C. U. Aitchison (ed.). A Collection of Treaties, Engagements, and Sunnuds Relating to India and Neighbouring Countries, vol. 2, Calcutta, 1876, pp. 166-168.
21. In V.K. Manandhar. A Documentary History of Nepalese Quinquennial Missions to China: 1792-1906, New Delhi, 2001, Appendix E, p. 5.
22. Ibid.
23. Ibid.
24. TNA, FO 766/6, Letter from the Nepalese Prime Minister Chandra Shum Shere to John Manners-Smith, 19 April, 1906, p. 6.
25. Ibid.
26. TNA, FO 535/14, India Office to Foreign Office, 11 March 1911, no. 16, p. 11; TNA, FO 535/14; Foreign Office to India Office, 15 March 1911, no. 18, p. 14; TNA, FO 535/14; Viscount Morley to Government of India, 28 March 1911, Encl. in no. 24, p. 19. The decision of the Government of India was communicated to Manners-Smith on 24 April, 1911; TNA, FO 535/14, Government of India to Lieutenant-Colonel Manners-Smith,24 April 1911, Encl. 2 in no. 63, p. 56.
27. Ibid.
28. Van Schaik, S. *Tibet: A History,* Yale University Press, London, 2011, pp. 1-3.
29. Ibid.
30. Ibid.
31. Ibid.
32. www.umass.edu/rso/fretibet/education.html accessed on 12 April 2016.
33. Muni, S.D. & Chadha, V. *Asian Strategic Review 2015: India as a Security Provider*, Pentagon Press, New Delhi, 2014, p. 112.
34. Ray, H. *China's strategy in Nepal,* Radiant Publishers, New Delhi, 1983, p. 122.
35. Wolfe, A. Nepal's Instability in the Regional Power Struggle, *Power and Interest News Report*, 3 February 2006 at http://www.worldproutassembly.org/archives/2006/02/nepals_instabil.html accessed on 30 July 2013.
36. Bhaumik, S. Guns, Drugs and Rebels, Seminar, issue 550, May 2005, at http://www.india-seminar. com/2005/550/550%20subir%20bhaumik.htm accessed on 12 April 2016.
37. Ghoble. China-Nepal Relations and India, *Asian Survey*, vol. 25, issue: 5, 1985, p. 23.
38. Sundaraman, S. The dragons teeth, *The Asian Age*, 15 December 2010 at http://archive.asianage.com/ columnists/dragon%E2%80%99s-teeth-535 accessed on 12 April 2016.
39. *Tibetan Review*, August 2008, pp. 23-24.
40. Bajpai, K. The Chinese Are Coming, *The Times of India*, 11 December 2010 at http://timesofindia.indiatimes.com/edit-page/The-Chinese-Are-Coming/articleshow/7078878.cms accessed on 21 May 2014.
41. Raman, B. Seeing China from Chengdu, South Asia Analysis Group (SAAG), vol. 2381, 2009, pp. 1-3.
42. Bhattacharya, A. Retrieved from http://www.idsa.in/idsastrategiccomments/ChinaslnroadsintoNepal_ABhattacharya_180509
43. Jaiswal, P. Caught in the India-China Rivalry: Policy options for Nepal, Institute of Peace and Conflict Studies, at http://www.ipcs.org/issue-brief/china/caught-in-the-india-china-rivalry-policy-options-for-nepal-249.html accessed on 30 August 2017.
44. Ibid.
45. Ibid.

5

India's Vulnerabilities and Growing Status in Asia and the World

India's Vulnerabilities

India's vulnerabilities in the next decade will be centred mainly in its neighbourhood. While the Indian subcontinent is a single geopolitical unit, it is fractured into several states, each with its own dynamics. As the largest country in the region, India's security concerns have always encompassed and will continue to encompass the entire subcontinent. This dictates a strategy that neutralises vulnerabilities inherent in these political divisions, specifically ensuring that India's neighbours do not become platforms for hostile activities against it by current or potential adversaries. Otherwise, India's ability to overcome an adverse, or leverage a potentially favourable, global environment will confront severe constraints. A brief understanding of India's role in South Asia becomes significant.

India's position in South Asia and its own perception of its immediate neighbourhood has seen innumerable policy shifts. The primary shift occurred with the end of the Cold War which necessitated a mutual security that emerged as against belonging to the umbrella of one great power or another. The second shift was discernible post India's nuclear test and its emergence as a declared nuclear power. Defence cooperation was enhanced in the form of joint military exercises. Indian Prime Minister Indira Gandhi, articulated in the *Foreign Affairs Journal* on India and the World: "We are not tied to the traditional concept of foreign policy designed to safeguard overseas possessions, investments, and carving out spheres of influence. We are not interested in exporting ideologies."

Later, India in 2005 confidently stated that it would prefer democracy though would not impose the same on any other country against the wishes of its people. Further, India also declared its willingness play a role of a security provider within the region. This was evident when the then Prime Minister Manmohan Singh, laying the foundation stone for the National Defence University in Gurgaon, said, "Our defence cooperation has grown and today we have unprecedented access to high technology, capital and partnerships.... We are well positioned, therefore, to become a net provider of security in our immediate region and beyond."

India's Ministry of Defence, however, on the other hand, was not seen as a reliable defence partner when it came to delivery of military equipment. India's domestic constraints severely crippled its external outreach and this was evident in the context of Nepal, Sri Lanka, and the Maldives where India watched with concern the blossoming defence cooperation of Nepal and Sri Lanka with Pakistan and China. New Delhi's inability to implement its promise to deliver lethal weapons, arms and ammunition to Nepal, Sri Lanka, and Afghanistan due to domestic compulsions severely crippled its role as a net security provider especially in the context of the strategic partnership that India has signed with Afghanistan and sought to sign with Nepal and later with Sri Lanka. Despite these domestic problems, India would have to assume a leadership role in the South Asian region. However, there will always be limits to its exercise of military power.

Indian and Chinese statesmen of the twentieth and early 21st century have ruminated at length on the grand vision of their two ancient Asian civilizations and now resurgent great neighbouring countries, becoming close partners, leading Asia and the world at large. After Indian independence in 1947, India emerged as the new leading power of Asia with Prime Minister Jawaharlal Nehru as the authentic voice of the whole "born-again Orient." Nehru had visited the Soviet Union in 1927 and China in 1939. He had told Kuomintang leader Chiang Kai-shek then, "More and more, I think of India and China pulling together in the future."

During the 1950s, India and China were in the Hindi-Chini Bhai-Bhai (India and China are brothers) honeymoon but it didn't last long.

By 1959, the two were at odds over the escape of the Dalai Lama to India and the granting of political asylum along with permission to allow him to create and run a Tibetan government-in-exile. There was also continuing acrimony over the McMahon Line that India had inherited from the British Colonial Empire. In 1962, India fought a brief war in the Himalayas with China, which India lost and shattered Nehru's vision of a common destiny. India was a neutral, non-aligned country, leaning towards the Soviet Union and China knew if it pushed India too hard it would risk a crisis or even military conflict with Moscow or drive India into the arms of the USA.

China had succeeded in downgrading India as the leading power of the non-aligned Afro-Asian world and during the 1960s and beyond forged a geo-political alliance with India's adversary, Pakistan, to keep India in check, have a backdoor to the outside world and outrun the US naval blockade of the Chinese Pacific east coast. The China-Pakistan axis became a strategic alliance, but China never intervened on Pakistan's behalf in its wars with India, or during the second Kashmir war in 1965 or in the Bangladesh independence war in 1971.

Post India's military victory over Pakistan and the resultant Bangladeshi independence, China withdrew political support for the Pakistani Kashmir policy and endorsed the signing in July 1972 by Indian Prime Minister Indira Gandhi and Pakistani President Zulfiqar Ali Bhutto of the Shimla Agreement which bound India and Pakistan to settle their differences by peaceful means through bilateral negotiations. Further, it accepted the Line of Control as the almost permanent international boundary. Till date, this agreement is the basis of all Chinese official pronouncements on the ongoing conflict.

Later, Deng Xiaoping, paramount leader of the People's Republic of China (1979-1989), stated in 1988 when he met the Indian Prime Minister, Rajiv Gandhi, during his visit to China. "The Asian age in the next century could only be realized if both India and China become developed economies." However, it took another 15 years for relations between the two countries to start improving. The Bush Administration had nominated India as a strategic partner for the containment of China, a concept that was supported by the Indian Right, but not accepted by the political party ruling India at that stage which was still married to India's tradition of a non-aligned nation following an independent foreign policy.

However, despite the optimism, no solution of the border conflict is in sight. India feels that China had started making excessive new demands, and Chinese think-tankers, who act as a weather vane for official Chinese government thinking, say that the irresponsible Indian media had created a wave of unjustified optimism that was now an obstacle to the negotiation process.

On the other hand, China had made a preliminary border settlement with Nepal, which provided clarity in recognition of its sovereignty. Nepal affirmed that an explicit friendship with China was part of its attempt to decrease dependency on India. While seeking to maintain equal friendship with both, Nepal also hoped that economic competition between them would enhance its own economic development. Economic opportunities with China, however, started seriously at the turn of the new millennium, and most particularly since the end of the People's War.

During a visit to China in August 1979, King Birendra, in his speech at the banquet in his honour, explained, "Nepal's foreign policy is founded on her desire to safeguard her independence and sovereignty and the related quest for peace. Our commitment to the institutionalization of peace in Nepal and our appreciation of your support for the objective is as strong as ever." Birendra was referring to China's positive response to the king's proposal of a Zone of Peace.

Management of our Neighbourhood

The management of our neighbourhood[1] which includes Nepal must enjoy the highest priority in the next decade. Episodic engagement and crisis management must yield place to a long-term focus on the following elements:[2]

(a) The economic integration of South Asia, with a willingness to implement significant and, if necessary, unilateral trade and economic liberalisation measures favouring our neighbours. This will give them a stake in India's growth and prosperity;

(b) Improving and upgrading connectivity among all countries of the region, through road, rail, air and electronic links. Without this infrastructure in place, regional economic integration will remain a chimera; and,

(c) Significantly expand cultural diplomacy to leverage the strong and enduring cultural and linguistic affinities we share with our neighbours.

The resilience India's economy has shown in the wake of the continuing global economic and financial crisis, positions her better than China since India's growth is largely domestic demand-driven and not linked to an artificially-maintained low exchange rate. In a landscape of several rising powers, India's rise is likely to be more sustainable than other largely export-driven economies.[3]

Various determinants of Indo-Nepalese relations have been examined. While some problems and irritants have been resolved, some continue to fester as before whereas others continue to grow to undesirable proportions. Both countries, given their peculiar internal dynamics and external compulsions, have tried to narrow down the gaps in their perceptions and sensitivities. However, much more needs to be done in this respect.

The year 2014 was when China became the world's biggest economy in purchasing power parity (PPP) terms, overtaking the USA for the first time in history. This move, which did not come as a surprise, is the sign of a superpower transition and gave evidence of the rising role of Asia on the international stage in what is already known as the Asian Century. It is largely believed that, Asia will continue to be the driving force in world economic growth. According to a recent report from the Asian Development Bank, India and some Asian economies are projected to grow at 6.4 per cent. Although continual regional cooperation tends to solidify Asia's position as the driver of global growth, perhaps a more telling tale is the growth of individual economies within the region.

Underpinning economic growth in Asia is not only the rise in domestic demand, particularly for middle-income countries such as Thailand and

Malaysia, but also an increase in foreign investment in less developed countries such as Cambodia, Laos, Myanmar, and Vietnam. The World Bank forecast an accelerated economic growth in South Asia driven by an increase in private investment and export activity in India.

Despite this impressive growth, Asia faces several major challenges. One is the uncertainty of China and India's growth outlook in the long-term and their capacity to implement policy reforms that will help them overcome their current deceleration in growth. For these Asian superpowers, as well as other economies across the region, the main challenges may very well be their capacity to overcome income inequality and to sustain their economies by adopting more environmentally friendly approaches.[4]

India's Vulnerability: Rising Inequality, Lower Economic Mobility

After decades of sustained economic growth that has led to a substantial reduction in poverty, India and Asia are experiencing new social tensions and economic vulnerabilities due to the global economic crisis, slower growth rates in emerging economies, concerns about water and food security, and weak or non-existent social safety nets. Rising inequalities and a growing demand for more equal opportunities make it imperative to think of economic growth in a more qualitative and inclusive manner, with not only less pronounced income gaps between the poor and the rich, but also better access to education and health, and more equal opportunities to benefit from the growth dividend. Both the inequalities within countries as well as the disparities across economies are threatening the long-term growth prospects of Asia.[5]

It is believed that Asia will overtake Europe in terms of its billionaire population, with a predicted 66 per cent growth in the number of the ultra-high-net-worth individuals (UHNWIs) – individuals with US$ 30 million or more in net assets, excluding their main residence – with the number of UHNWIs expected to grow by 80 per cent in China, 99 per cent in India, 144 per cent in Indonesia, and a whopping 166 per cent in Vietnam. However, at the micro-economic level, rising inequalities mean lower economic and social mobility. This manifests in the inability of younger generations to earn more over their lifetime, or earn more than their parents did at a similar age. It also means fewer opportunities for the economies to benefit from the talents and economic contributions of the majority. At the macro-economic level, disparities among countries are also impeding the economic capacity of the region. For economies like Thailand and Malaysia, the threat of the middle-income trap is real. It is clear that lack of innovation, low investments in technology and education, rising labour costs, and stagnant productivity risk are preventing or delaying these middle-income economies from shifting towards a higher-productivity economic structure.[6]

For India, stronger regional economic cooperation, including through SAARC and ASEAN, will be essential to achieve more equitable and inclusive growth.[7] Public and private initiatives to increase intra-regional trade, ensure competitive business environments, attract foreign and domestic investment, and integrate small and medium enterprises (SMEs) into regional and global value chains should be made easier by the rise of Asian-led multilateral banks, the proliferation of free trade agreements, and progressive social policies that contribute to the region's growth. The region will also need to confront a host of mounting environmental challenges, including rapid environmental degradation, resource scarcity, and climate change. These problems compound the difficulty of reducing inequality, since they disproportionately affect the poorest and most vulnerable groups. In response, more countries are recognizing the need to transit to green growth strategies, incorporating environmental considerations into their national development plans to foster low-emission and sustainable, as well as socially inclusive, development. Sustainably managing resources can also serve as an important driver of growth, allowing countries to gain a competitive edge and spur greater job creation and prosperity.

The Asia-Pacific region is now the world's largest user of natural resources. The regions rapid industrial development and export-led growth model has relied heavily on fossil fuel-intensive infrastructure and the exploitation of its natural resource base. This has led to a sharp rise in resource use and emissions in the Asia-Pacific – which continues to grow at a faster rate than any other region – as well as high levels of pollution and resource depletion. The economic impact of this can be staggering. In China, for instance, environmental degradation is estimated to cost the country approximately 9 per cent of its gross national income, according to the World Bank. At the same time, domestic consumption in Asia continues to expand, creating an unprecedented demand for more energy, clean water, and natural resources. If current rates of depletion continue, competition for resources will intensify.[8]

Experts feel that the Indian economy will remain vulnerable to changes in the world's climate, which is expected to cause extreme weather, inland and coastal flooding, rising sea levels, heat stress, and famine. The Asian Development Bank also estimates that climate change damage could reduce economic growth in South Asia alone by 9 per cent annually by 2100. Warmer weather will adversely affect food production, causing it to drop in Bangladesh, Bhutan, India, and Sri Lanka by as much as 23 per cent and increase food insecurity for the poor.[9]

These environmental challenges are often exacerbated by well-intentioned but harmful economic policies, such as fuel subsidies that encourage people to turn to inefficient, polluting forms of energy. In the past, many policymakers also remained sceptical on whether they could implement environmental-friendly policies without causing economic growth rates to drop. As many of these challenges transcend national boundaries, they provide an opportunity for greater regional cooperation. Governments not only need to include environmental considerations in their notion of sustainable economic growth, but also collaborate at the regional level to manage resources, reduce pollution, and increase energy efficiency.

Asia is still home to two-thirds of the world's poor and economic growth both domestically and regionally must include the poorest, most vulnerable and disadvantaged. Increasing demand and rapid urbanization are causing major constraints for resources in large populated areas, and as such pose a risk to the environment and emphasize the need for nations to seriously tackle the adverse impacts of climate change. Regional cooperation has the potential for creating a marketplace for better-quality products at lower prices, better connectivity, reduced costs of production, and increased job opportunities, provided it is managed in a way that is conducive to a sound and transparent business environment. It also has the potential for greater vulnerability of the poorest if not well managed.[10]

To be successful in the long-term, regional cooperation will have to focus on more inclusive and sustainable growth. Similarly, in order to meet the ambitious post-2015 Sustainable Development Goals, governments, policymakers, social and economic actors, as well as the international community, will need to pay as much attention to regional challenges and regional governance as to domestic ones. If Asia can closely integrate as a regional bloc while moving towards a more inclusive and sustainable future, then the 21st century will definitely be the Asian Century.[11]

Reality Check on Relations with Nepal

The dilemma which India faces is that those with whom it has good equations have failed to perform well during the elections. With those that have done well in the elections in Nepal, India has a trust deficit. India needs to resolve this dilemma and move ahead.[12]

Reintegrating the Subcontinent

India needs a reality check on its relations with Nepal, with whom its security is closely linked. Events post-Jana Andolan II, the Constituent Assembly elections and the promulgation of the constitution has markedly changed the political scenario in Nepal and this has had its impact on Indo-Nepal relations. The Maoists too face a contradiction, though they speak of equidistance with regard to China and India in policy, they hesitatingly and in camera, accept that in reality, it is not so. Of the 40 demands which the Maoists had put forward in 2007 during the insurgency days, most were directly or indirectly related to grievances with India.[13]

The rapid rise of China is the single most important geopolitical development of our time. The consequences of China's emergence at the top of the international system is likely to unfold throughout the 21st century. Yet, it has not been easy to come to terms with the prospect that one of India's closest Asian neighbours is on the way to becoming a superpower. As a result, there has been little debate about the meaning of the rise of China and its long-term implications for India's foreign and national security policies. India's debate on China continues to oscillate between crude formulations of the China threat or romantic notions about Sino-Indian cooperation as reflected in the idea of Chindia (China-India). The anxieties about China's assertive policies have comprehensively enveloped India's policy makers, and this will only rise further.[14]

Although China is already India's largest trading partner and the two nations are neighbours, the level of contact and communication between the two governments and societies remains way below potential. As a consequence, there is profound ignorance about each other across the two nations. As it promotes more intensive engagement with Beijing, Delhi must take major steps to promote the study of China in all its dimensions by the Indian business and political classes.

As India reaffirms its political commitment to move forward on a boundary settlement, it needs to look at China beyond the prism of bilateral relations, for the rise in Chinese power is affecting India's foreign policy across the board. From the reorganization of major international organizations to India's relations with its South Asian neighbours, and from the bilateral competition for natural resources in Africa to securing influence in the remote islands of the South Pacific, New Delhi, and Beijing are constantly stepping on each other's toes. India cannot address the challenge by simply raising the spectre of a China threat or attributing malevolent intent to all aspects of China's policy for its own growth and security.[15]

The rise in Beijing's influence across the world, including in India's own immediate neighbourhood is an inevitable consequence of China's rapidly increasing weight in the global economy and polity. There is no way India can alter this trend. New Delhi should focus instead on revamping its own foreign policy and security to make it more effective in the subcontinent and her extended neighbourhood in Africa, Asia and the Indian Ocean littoral.

In a world of many super powers, India could be the potential swing state that defines the balance of power in the system and build on the advantages that derive from it. On the other hand, India is also vulnerable to shifting alignments and realignments among the great powers. For example, India is wary of a Sino-US Cold War that might compel it to make choices it is not ready to make. At the same time, India is equally anxious about a Sino-American condominium or G-2 that will severely constrain India's room for manoeuvre.[16]

Navigating a multi-polar world demands less emphasis on preconceived ideological slogans alongside a diplomatic agility that allows India to respond effectively to the shifting balance of power dynamics in the world. Delhi must continue to strive for a lasting partnership with the USA that is far removed from our borders, build new partnerships with Japan and Europe, sustain traditional links with Russia, manage the complex dynamic with neighbouring China, and ensure against a hostile alignment of these powers against India's interests in one or more issue areas. Most important of all, India must continue to improve her relationship with her neighbours.[17]

India has also steadily fallen behind China in the area of infrastructure diplomacy in Asia. While China's plans to build north-south transport corridors in Asia are moving forward, India's proposals on east-west corridors through Burma (now Myanmar) and Thailand have languished. India must make the construction of the Hanoi-Delhi and Singapore-Kolkata transport corridors as high priority projects in Prime Minister Narendra Modi's term. Japan, which is looking at such linkages and is helping India build the Delhi-Mumbai corridor, could be a natural partner in India's infrastructure diplomacy.[18]

Over the past two decades, India has demonstrated its ability to carry out underground nuclear tests and its capability to deliver nuclear warheads using intermediate ballistic missiles. However, it has not yet utilised these newly acquired capabilities to project power effectively. Regionally, a large percentage of India's Armed Forces are stationed along the country's extensive border areas with Pakistan and China. This inefficient allocation of military resources has limited India's power projection beyond its borders. In addition, the focus on India's modest nuclear capabilities has detracted attention from weaknesses in India's conventional forces. For instance, India does not have a strong weapons manufacturing industry, so it imports an overwhelming amount of its sophisticated military hardware from abroad, mostly from Russia. Moreover, India's existing conventional military equipment is in severe need of modernisation.[19]

Given the massive challenge of domestic poverty and under-development, India simply has not had the resources to enable the development of a modern military arsenal. As such, it has been unable to assert itself on the international stage. In international conflicts, India's military has only been active in humanitarian assistance and ancillary non-combat roles.[20]

In the debate on Asian institutional architecture, there are warning signs that New Delhi must wake up to. Although India became a member of the 18-nation East Asia Summit (EAS), China has succeeded in ensuring the primacy of the ASEAN-Plus Three (APT) Association. Growing trade and economic cooperation in northeast Asia, between China, Japan, and Korea is also overshadowing the prospects for an ASEAN-led integration. This, in turn, would suggest that merely tailing ASEAN is not an adequate policy for India in East Asia. Sustained economic growth and successful consolidation of its democracy are making Indonesia a powerful force in the region and a natural ally of India.[21]

India's institutions are a long way from responding to the growing interest in military and security collaboration with New Delhi. Emphasizing security partnerships and delivering on such cooperation must be at the very top of a rejuvenated Look East policy.[22]

Since India is a democratic state, the elected government will have to be responsive to the demands of its citizens and this will ensure that the existing pressure for the redistribution of wealth will restrict growth in military expenditure and as a consequence, inhibit the ability of the state to turn India into a global power.

Nepal as one of India's closest neighbours must remain a priority. Her geographical location is also very important for India's defence. Due to its strategic importance for Indian defence from China to the north, the British during their colonial rule had done everything to transform Nepal into a friendly buffer state between China and British possessions in India. Post the British rule of India, the post-colonial government of India had also taken note of Nepal's strategic importance and quickly signed a Treaty of Peace and Friendship covering all aspects of Nepal-India relations in 1950, followed by a letter of exchange. Similarly, both countries concluded an agreement on arms procurement in 1965 and in 1978 India agreed to sign a trade and transit treaty with landlocked Nepal.[23]

There are some genuine and legitimate concerns on India's security viewpoint on Nepal. While Nepal pursues its foreign policy, it is of utmost importance for Nepal to consider these security concerns of India. It is also important to note that while giving due consideration for India's security concerns, it does not mean that Nepal has to compromise its sovereignty and independent stance and neutral foreign policies which Indian policy makers often seem to demand from Nepal. About Indian security concerns, the expressions made by Indian leaders from time to time have become quite controversial. When Prime Minister Nehru in 1950 said, Nepal is geographically almost a part of India, although she is an independent country, prominent Nepalese found this statement paternalistic and even interpreted it as Indian attempt to undermine Nepal's sovereign and independent status. It is also a fact that Nepal's relations with India and its access to the sea port in Kolkata, which is about 1,000 kilometres away, and also her southern border connection is easier to traverse than the vastness and difficult terrain of Tibet's mountainous lands. This dependence can be leveraged but seeing it as a liability implies an inability to treat Nepal as a somewhat equal nation. It is important to note here that on the other hand, Nepal has to be sensitive in not allowing its land to be used by any anti-Indian forces and provide better confidence to the Indian side and should not allow any activities that undermine the Indian security sensitivity.

Similarly, Nepal has to be equally sensitive about not allowing any anti-Tibet or anti-Chinese activities on Nepalese soil. The Tibet Autonomous Region (TAR) of China, is also a strategically important location for extending China's relations with South Asia. TAR is regarded as China's Achilles Heel where a large number of anti-Chinese elements have identified inimical interests. Nepal, therefore, needs to be sensitive about the Tibetan situation and possible misuse of Nepalese land by those anti-Chinese forces. Post the establishment of the Nepal-China diplomatic relationship in 1955, relations between two countries have been regarded as friendly and cordial and both countries have resolved their existing border dispute. At present, there are no contentious issues that are likely to create problems in the near future between these two countries. China's concern in Nepal is Tibet and its security, and any trouble, especially in the areas of security and instability in Nepal, would strengthen anti-China elements on its borders. The Khampa uprising of the 1960s and 1970s[24] was a sensitive issue for the Chinese in the past. Over the last few decades, Khampa activities have been contained; however, they may not have completely died out/stopped. Chinese are concerned that Nepal should not to be a springboard for anti-Chinese forces/activity. As an emerging global power, China's interest is not only to secure its borders but also to seek stable, cordial and friendly relations with its immediate neighbours. A country which cannot secure stable relationships with its neighbours and maintain stability, cannot hope for legitimate international status. Therefore, the geographical location of Nepal is of grave and important interest to both her neighbours and any instability within Nepal would be a matter of concern.

A series of political and military crises in different parts of South Asia and the rapidly expanding role of China in our neighbourhood have raised awareness in New Delhi for the need for the institution of a comprehensive security strategy towards her neighbourhood. During the last two decades, India's previous two prime ministers, Atal Bihari Vajpayee and Manmohan Singh, emphasized the importance of recasting India's South Asian policy. They highlighted the need for a peaceful periphery, offered unilateral economic concessions to neighbours, unveiled plans for the modernization of the border infrastructure, promised to resolve long-standing bilateral political disputes, and accelerated the pace of regional integration. Although the government moved on all these fronts, the pace and scope were never enough to cope with the rapidity of the regions political evolution and the momentum behind China's rising profile in South Asia.

Over the next few years, Delhi will have to move much faster to sustain India's primacy in the South Asian region. While the government must continue to focus on political engagement with its neighbours and trade liberalization, Delhi must enlist the corporate sector as well as leverage the connections that the Indian Armed Forces have been able to establish within the neighbourhood to boost Indian diplomacy in the region. Without significant Indian private investment in the neighbouring countries that can produce exportable goods to our markets, there is no way trade with our neighbours can be expanded in an equitable manner. Without a visible balance in trade and a linkage with the armed forces of these countries, which in many of our neighbouring countries are decision shapers, it would be difficult to generate the requisite political support across the borders for security and economic integration with the larger Indian security and economic infrastructure. This would demand that Delhi create well-funded special vehicles for addressing the security concerns of our neighbourhood as well as push Indian investments in the neighbouring countries and generous market access to goods produced with Indian inputs. That will rapidly boost two-way trade with our neighbours and create enduring constituencies across the borders for security and economic cooperation with India.

Linked to this must be a larger role for the private sector in partnership with central and state governments in the modernization of trade facilities all along our borders. Major Indian corporations must also be encouraged to undertake trans-border mega projects in collaboration with international entities to depoliticise trans-border infrastructural cooperation with our neighbours. Building modern transport links with our neighbours is the key to progress and the negotiations on these are held up because of the traditional emphasis on inter-governmental negotiations. By minimizing the direct role of governments and thereby reducing the political incentives for standing up against India, New Delhi will make it easier for our neighbours to do what is in their own enlightened self-interest. By encouraging the private sector to take the lead on trans-border economic cooperation, the government will be able to focus more sharply on political and security cooperation with our neighbours, modernize the outdated bilateral treaty arrangements, and checkmate hostile activities by rival powers in India's neighbourhood.

The individual person is at the origin of all economic activity. The individuals personal and cultural traits decide how and with whom he or she interacts economically. Whereas personal characteristics may be assumed to be purely random, cultural traits are not; the latter may have an important impact on economic behaviour.[25] Therefore, cultural and ethnic links are also very important in discussing the geopolitical aspects of a country. Present-day Nepal in the Central Himalayan represents an area of the interface of two culture worlds and is a meeting point for two specific countries and civilizations, India and China, and for two regions, South Asia and Central Asia.[26]

Despite all this, the promise of a brighter future for India still holds firm. There are three reasons for this:

Economic: Prime Minister Modi's initiatives aimed at revamping India's restrictive business regulations and creating a real free market seem to be working. Even though GDP growth has slowed slightly India's US$ 1.9 trillion economy is projected to expand by 6.4 per cent over the next couple of years, according to the International Monetary Fund, and the country has already outpaced Japan as the world's third largest economy in terms of purchasing price parity, a measure that adjusts for price differences between economies, according to the World Bank. In addition, falling oil prices have reduced the risk of inflation and will enable the country to cut its costly fuel subsidies. Every US$ 10-a-barrel decline could increase GDP by 0.1 per cent, lower inflation by 0.5 per cent, and narrow the current account deficit. Further bolstering the economy are the billions of dollars in increased foreign investments, including US$ 33 billion from private and public sources in Japan, aided by the raising of investment caps by the government and a stable interest rate environment.

Infrastructure: The second part of Prime Minister Modi's plan is to improve India's national infrastructure. This includes a proposed increase in infrastructure spending of US$ 800 billion to reach a targeted economic growth of seven per cent as well as enable banks to buy infrastructure bonds to spur trading activity in the debt markets. Prime Minister Modi secured a US$ 20 billion infrastructure investment from China. Collectively, these initiatives could enable India to upgrade its overtaxed transport system, bring stable water supply and electricity to more areas, and expand the use of technology throughout the country. However, the most important aspect of India's infrastructure is its human capital. What makes India's population so valuable is its large pool of young workers. At present, 65 per cent of India's population is 35 or under, giving the country a strong competitive edge in the coming decades.[27] To realize the potential of this human capital, the government has launched several initiatives aimed at improving education, re-training rural workers for skilled jobs in other sectors, providing bank accounts to all Indians to teach personal financial planning, offering free life insurance, encouraging the wider use of computers and the Internet, and generally modernizing the workforce for the big job boom coming up in the fast-growing healthcare, information technology, telecom, and retail sectors.

Geopolitical: The final factor that could position India as a superpower is its geopolitical advantage. India has made concerted efforts to strengthen ties with Russia, Japan, and the USA. For each of them, India is a valuable trading partner with a vast consumer base and labour pool waiting to be tapped. Even more significant is the strategic importance of its alliance with all those nations. As far as Russia is concerned, it is reeling under Western economic sanctions and low oil prices; realistically Russia needs India's partnership more than ever to bolster its economic foothold in Asia and counter US influence. Similarly, the USA would like to expand bilateral trade with India, while also using the democratic nation to balance the power of China in the region. By extending the hand of friendship to all of them, it is thought that Prime Minister Modi is being diplomatic; but he is also keeping his options open to forge partnerships that will maximize the benefit to India, both financially and politically.[28]

Therefore, it is felt that India may not reach its desired destination in a straight line or in a particular timeframe that many so-called decision shapers may have set for it, but there is no doubt that in the long run, the odds are pretty good that India will become a leading player in the economic and geopolitical spheres in the near future.

India-Nepal Socio-Religious Connect

Nepal is the host country of two major religions, Hinduism and Buddhism, and these religions are the most dominant religions of both India and China, respectively. Nepal is wedged between India in the south and Tibet and China in the North, and this intermediary position has had a definite bearing on the development of her culture and way of life. India and Chinese Tibet were the two countries which have influenced Nepal culturally and since cultural and religious ties and commonalities are stronger than the geographical proximities or other economic interests there is a great deal of commonality of interests.

Nepal's northern region is inhabited by immigrants from Tibet and the southern region by the people of Indian origin. The Nepalese of the Terai region, who are of Indian origin and predominantly Hindus, have linguistic, cultural and religious bonds with the people of India. Similarly, the people of the upper hills and mountain region are of Mongoloid stock, share closer cultural, linguistic and religious ties with the people of Tibet and China. Thus, Nepal is a meeting point for two civilizations. Both the regions of Nepal especially in the south, due to the open border and accessible land, have strong ties with the neighbouring Indian districts and states of Bihar, Uttar Pradesh, and West Bengal.[29]

Each year hundreds of thousands of Indian Hindu pilgrims visit Pashupatinath temple in Kathmandu and also a large number of Nepali pilgrims cross the border to visit Indian temples. In the border area, there are a large number of Nepalese people who have family ties with people in the northern Indian states such as Bihar, Uttar Pradesh, and West Bengal. Such close cultural links of these two countries have also been promoted by other social and educational exchanges. It is common practice, especially for Nepalese students, to receive higher education and training in India.[30] A large number of Nepalese work as a migrant labour in different parts of India. Similarly, a number of Indian origin or in some cases, citizens, though in much lesser strength, work in Nepal in various fields such as teachers, shopkeepers and also run Nepal-based businesses.

India-Nepal Historical-Political Connect

Historically, the political relationship of the leaders of post-Rana Nepal and newly independent India is another determinant factor for this deep political friendship between the two countries. The political leaders have shared deep personal and political association. A large number of Nepalese politicians were educated in India especially since there were no facilities for higher education in Nepal during the Rana oligarchy period of 1846-1950.[31] During their student time in India, many Nepalese leaders were put in Indian jails for their participation in India's freedom movement against British colonialism. The two dominant political parties of Nepal (the Nepali Congress and the Communist Party of Nepal) were established in India in the late forties and they launched their pro-democracy movement in Nepal whilst they were still in exile in India. This had helped to develop a close personal and political association and bond between the leaders of the two countries. P.R. Sharma, a renowned Nepalese writer, pointed out that the comradeship between the leaders of the two countries had a great bearing on relations of both countries when these Nepalese leaders occupied positions in the government after the overthrow of the Ranas in the 1950s.[32]

The northern Himalayas and the mountains were the natural borders for the protection of Nepal; the malaria-prone jungle in the south similarly warded off any southern-based invasion/foreign penetration. With this very natural geographical barrier, Nepal's position as a buffer state was secure. However, with the eradication of malaria and construction of various roads and the migration of people from the hills to the southern plains, this natural buffer has been compromised. Numerous roads and entry points were built to connect India to enhance economic, trade, cultural, educational, and political permeability of Nepal which, as a consequence, reduced its natural frontiers with India.

NOTES

1. Saran, S. Premature power, *Business Standard*, 17 March 2010 at http://www.business-standard.com/article/opinion/shyam-saran-premature-power-110031700019_1.html accessed on 2 August 2016.
2. Ibid.
3. Ibid.
4. Ibid.

5. Ibid.
6. Ibid.
7. Ibid.
8. Ibid.
9. Ibid.
10. Ibid.
11. Ibid.
12. Murthy, P. Time to Reassess Indo-Nepal Relations, Institute of Peace and Conflict Studies, issue 2965, September 2009 at http://www.ipcs.org/article/south-asia/time-to-reassess-indo-nepal-relations-2965.html accessed on 2 August 2016.
13. Ibid.
14. Aspen Institute India. Changing Priorities: New Dimensions of India's Foreign Policy & National Security, 15-16 February, 2012 at http://www.anantaaspencentre.in/pdf/changing_priorities.pdf accessed on 12 March 2015.
15. Ibid.
16. Mohan, C.R. Diplomacy for the new decade, January 2010 at http://www.india-seminar.com/2010/605/605_c_raja_mohan.htm accessed on 30 August 2017.
17. Ibid.
18. Ibid.
19. Jack Neenan (2018). India will never become a superpower,, 11 January 2018, *SOAS blog*
20. Ibid.
21. Ibid.
22. Ibid.
23. Bhattari, R. Geopolitical specialties of Nepal and international approach to conflict transformation at http://nepalforeignaffairs.com/geopolitical-specialties-of-nepal-and-international-approach-to-conflict-transformation/ accessed on 30 August 2017.
24. Fjeld, H. The rise of the Polyandrous House: Marriage, Kinship and Social Mobility in Rural Tsang, Tibet, October 2006, University of Oslo, unpublished thesis.
25. Helble, M. On The Influence of World Religions on International Trade, Graduates Institute of International Studies. University of Geneva, Switzerland, 2007, pp. 2-3.
26. Bhattari, R. Geopolitical specialties of Nepal and international approach to conflict transformation, *Nepal Foreign Affairs*, January 2005 at http://nepalforeignaffairs.com/geopolitical-specialties-of-nepal-and-international-approach-to-conflict-transformation/ accessed on 30 July 2013.
27. Sanjay Sanghoee. India the next Super Power, *Fortune*, 25 January 2015,
28. Ibid.
29. Ibid.
30. Ibid.
31. Ibid.
32. Bhattari, R. Retrieved from http://nepalforeignaffairs.com/geopolitical-specialities-of-nepal-and-international-approach-to-conflict-transformation.

6

SUMMARY AND RECOMMENDATIONS

Two dominant perceptions do, in fact, mirror a great deal of truth about existing bilateral relations. Dwelling on Nepal-India relations in his autobiography, ***Atmabrittanta (Late Life Recollections)***, Nepal's former Prime Minister B.P. Koirala has very aptly explained, "Our ties shouldn't be interpreted only on the basis of ancient history and culture. Look at Europe; it may be one culturally, but they were always fighting and killing each other. Distrust does not disappear just because there is cultural affinity. Relationships are dependent upon differing perspectives on society and differing expectations of the future. These manifests how, despite centuries of shared past, the relations between these nations are complex."

The Treaty of Peace and Friendship concluded between India and Nepal in July 1950 was intended to be an instrument of bilateral cooperation between the two countries, but opposition to this treaty and demands to review/revoke it have been made since the early 1950s. The Nepalese describe it as an unequal and one-sided agreement which endangered the sovereignty of Nepal. It is, therefore, important to analyse the reasons for Nepali opposition to the treaty, their fears, and concerns and how these could be removed, especially given the widespread anti-India sentiments erupting in protests over the years. At the same time, it is also important that Nepal recognize the possible threat that its international policies may impose on India's security which resulted in India not supporting some of its policies.

In India's dealings with Nepal, it is desirable to establish a more equitable relationship. India needs to accept that there are now new important players in Nepal who have the legitimacy and approval of the people at large. These players look at interdependence and bilateral relations in a different paradigm which need not necessarily be anti-India.[1] Channels of communication with all these political parties need to be cultivated, for their views will define the Nepal of the future. Economically, India must continue to give Nepal latitude due to the existing economic asymmetry between the two countries. The border must be well monitored jointly with infrastructural and support facilities provided by India.

The central hypothesis of this book is that despite existing age-old relations, shared culture, religion, economic and political closeness and a common destiny, permanent fault lines remain, and that these should not be allowed to fester and grow, especially since they have a direct bearing on the security of the Indian heartland. India's policy must be continually adjusted and fine-tuned according to newer and more demanding circumstances so as to ensure that India and Nepal remain partners in progress and do not get mired in any permanent conflict.

What is in India's best interests? A stable Nepal is India's highest priority.[2] The failure to move forward towards the framing of a constitution is the single-most destabilising factor in Nepal today. Regardless of the anti-India rhetoric emerging from various political parties in Nepal from time to time, even such dissenting parties also often seek India's support during periods of crisis and India too has always tried to keep that commitment towards maintaining mutual ties, which, in turn, is reflective of an inherent awareness of the age-old relations that always existed between these nations. This feeling of closeness and affinity between these nations should be continued and the bonds strengthened, which is possible only when both the governments are politically well aligned. Thus, it serves both India's and Nepal's best interests when there exists stability in Nepal's governance in particular and society at large.

Two consistent but very dominant perceptions characterise Nepal-India relations. The first considers these relations rooted, among others, in similarities of culture, tradition, religion, geography and the way of life and these unique similarities are viewed as having great strength and virtues of an enduring nature. India is held as Nepal's closest of friends, a friend that has always stood by Nepal's side in troubled times. Occasional swings in relations are taken as natural because of the intensive and extensive nature of these relations. The underpinnings of relations are believed to be strong enough to withstand any occasional ups and downs. It is generally stressed that both countries must continue to strive for the consolidation of the foundation of these relations in the light of the changing needs of time and to expand them further into more mutually beneficial areas of cooperation.

Concurrently, the counter view takes India as a country still carrying an imperial legacy and haunted by the colonial mindset, always wanting to keep its smaller neighbours under its sphere of influence and its conduct has never matched its stated commitment to friendship. It is often wondered, in this view, whether India is Nepal's true and well-meaning friend as it always professes, or does it merely want to perennially expand its political, social and economic footprints in Nepal, even if it means creating constant regime changes through the creation of multiple power centres?

On 20 September 2015, Nepal's new constitution was passed, amid violent protests by Madhesi and Tharu groups across the southern Terai plains that continued for months, leaving 57 dead. Protesting groups said the statute backtracked on addressing structural discrimination. The protests had deep support in ethnic Madhesi Terai communities, reflecting a profound, increasing sense of alienation from the state. A 135-day blockade of vital supplies by Madhesi civic and political groups, ended with no political solution on the table. It is likely therefore that the protests are almost certain to resume. To stop violent polarisation and a breakdown of social relations, Nepalese national parties, and other protesting groups must urgently agree on how to manage contentious issues, with timelines, guarantees, and a role for civic participation. A sustainable, equitable social contract is necessary for lasting peace and reconciliation.

After the devastating earthquakes in Spring 2015, the largest parties in the Nepalese Constituent Assembly decided, amid controversy, to fast-track a new constitution so as to fulfil a longstanding peace process commitment and enable them to focus on reconstruction. Some administrative and structural reforms mandated by the 2006 Comprehensive Peace Agreement (CPA), 2007 Interim Constitution and other political agreements are enshrined in the new constitution. However, Madhesi, Tharu, Jana Jati, Dalit, religious minorities and women's groups, considered historically marginalised, believed that the new statute and the process by which it was rushed through diluted commitments to meaningful federalism, redress for historical, structural discrimination based on ethnic and religious identity and gender, and democratic consultation was flawed and there is disagreement over boundaries of new states, electoral representation and affirmative action, constituency delineation and citizenship-related clauses. Supporters of the new constitution feel much has already been achieved and claim an excessive focus on identity-based grievances threatens Nepal's unity, integrity; even sovereignty.

The objections of those who demonstrated against it have their roots in long-running social disagreements on what it means to be Nepali and whether a homogenous conception of Nepal has led to structural discrimination against groups that do not conform to the behaviour and values of hill-origin, Nepali-speaking, upper-caste Hindu communities.

The blockade was an extreme form of protest with complex consequences, including grievous harm to the weakest and poorest sections of Nepali society and alienating communities the protestors should have been making common cause with. Yet, judging it to be a failure as a tactic should not be a substitute for a careful assessment of what is, in effect, a social movement in the Terai. All political parties and most protesters agree that the way forward is to amend the new constitution, not scrap it. In January 2016, the major parties passed two amendments related to more inclusive representation in state institutions and delineation of constituencies. Madhesi parties and protestors say these do not adequately address their grievances. Like the constitution, they were adopted unilaterally by the largest parties, losing the legitimacy they would have had as the outcome of a political negotiation.

Positions are not irreconcilable, but the prerequisites for any solution – respect, trust, political will, and a degree of selflessness, are in short supply.

There is a clear risk of escalating violence in the Terai. The depth of social discontent, lack of fruitful negotiations and disillusion with Madhesi parties are creating room for radical positions. Mainstream national parties are also in the Terai, and some are inclined to launch counter protests, which are likely to lead to violent clashes. The security forces are seen as discriminating against Madhesis and had been accused of using excessive force against them. Employing them repeatedly to quell local protests fuels anger and radicalisation and could encourage armed Madhesi groups, of which the region has a history, and might also allow a fringe Madhesi secessionist movement to gain traction. While unlikely to be successful or widespread, it would increase the volatility of a complex region. If implementation begins before these issues are addressed, the mainstream parties risk wholesale rejection of the constitution by a large section of the population. Discussions are ongoing in the government about conducting local elections; these too carry grave risks of violence, boycotts, intimidation and, in some areas, rejection of the state and its political system.

The vision of Nepal as a functioning, tolerant, forward-looking, multi-ethnic society presented in the agreements that were reached after the armed conflict between the Maoist movement and the state ended is in crisis. Those documents are the basis of today's polity and cannot be replaced unilaterally. Forcing acceptance of a flawed constitution could end the political transition and trigger another unmanageable new conflict.

India needs to decide to what extent it is in the interest of India to extend its assistance to change in the political affairs of Nepal. There is much to do bilaterally on the environmental, cultural, and economic fronts. There is a grave danger of Nepal being constantly insecure and on the boil. This would open Nepal up to the possibility of societal instability leading to similar disturbances in adjacent Indian States.

There would also be a need to consider the economic impact constant political instability in Nepal would have on the dispossessed northern regions of Bihar and Uttar Pradesh. The existing open border creates such an interconnected socio-cultural web that a stable and prosperous Nepal will be a catalyst for this region; likewise, an unstable Nepal can wreak havoc.

The weakness of Nepal studies within Indian academia is astounding, and can only be the result of overwhelming preoccupation of the academia at large to dabble with the larger geopolitics of the world, with little interest in the welfare of India's own peripheral populations. India needs to deepen its study of Nepal. An understanding of the geography, demography, economy, the democratic urge of the citizenry, as well as the history of the oldest and non-colonised nation-state of South Asia makes Nepal (comparatively) a different kind of country within South Asia. At present, India's focus seems exclusively geo-strategic, to do with countenancing China across the Himalayan range. This exclusive preoccupation must be reviewed because of the transformed ground realities where much has changed in terms of aspirations and access to information on all sides.[3]

In today's fast-paced world, the transforming economy, terrain, and geopolitics of the people residing in the central Himalayas demand an evolved doctrine of engagement with Nepal, even for India's self-interest. A new world is beckoning, far different from when India's doctrine on the Himalayan rim land was encoded in the early 1960s. Environmental stresses have increased right along the Himalayan chain over the past half century, and human intervention is drastic, as seen in the violence done to the Teesta's flow in Sikkim or in the construction of roads in Nepal. The entire Himalayas and the plains of the Ganga make up one single ecosystem, requiring geophysical sensitivity, even more than geopolitical. Certainly it is time for India to get over the perfunctory tags of who is pro-Indian and pro-Chinese, a simplistic formulation which hurts only oneself vis-à-vis the need for nuance in international relations. At a time when the Chinese railway network has arrived on the Tibetan plateau and threatens to move further into Nepal, there is need to ensure and facilitate Nepal's need to ease its landlocked-ness by extending highway connectivity northwards from India, especially when the Indian economy itself stands to benefit with these additional connects.

Vitally, there is the need to plan and increase cross-border linkages and projects related to natural resources, whether and what kind of dams and reservoirs are to be built; evaluating embankments along the main rivers for the silt they trap; the environmental dangers to both sides from excavation of the Chure (Shivalik) hills to feed India's need for rocks and boulders; or the meaning of receding glaciers (mainly the result of the South Asian brown cloud) for the entire downstream region.[4]

Nepal and India need to discuss regulating the open bilateral border without compromising its status as the most naturally evolved frontier of the region. Kathmandu needs to consider the social security of the uncounted but more than five million Nepali citizens working in India, while New Delhi must address the vulnerabilities of Indian citizens of Nepali origin, as well as Indians working north of the border. How will the introduction of biometric ID cards in India impact the status of Nepali citizens working legally under the umbrella of the 1950 Treaty of Peace and Friendship, and can Nepal's own upcoming national ID card help in managing the movement of citizenry?[5]

From public health to a shared security paradigm, to a shared economic growth, promoting tourism without borders to developing mutual academic depth, Nepal and India must work as one.[6] There has to be a rebuilding of empathy and trust between the two governments, which must start by rolling back the hyper-activism of the media and rebuilding of relationships between the politicians of two sides, between the armies of both nations, between the ex-soldiers of Nepal who have served India and are more than willing to serve and assist India again.[7]

Recommendations

From an earlier primary survey, I had observed that the Indian Army ex-servicemen of Nepali origin (respondents) have always held the country for which they fought and many gave their lives for (India) in great esteem and want to assist in improving Indo-Nepal relations and the issues that surround it. They were satisfied with their service in the Indian Army and the pension that they are being provided, which allows them the means to fulfil their economic requirements as well as those of their families. They continue to hold a good opinion of India and favour India as compared to other neighbouring nations. However, they also felt that India does interfere in the domestic politics of Nepal. Thus, it is important that while dealing with Indo-Nepal relations, such issues be dealt with taking into consideration all the above-mentioned factors covered in the survey. What was also clear from this survey was that the 125,000, Nepali origin Indian Army ex-servicemen community continues to be solidly behind India and would definitely assist if the need arose and if called upon to do so. They also stated that they had never been approached by either the Indian Army or the Indian Embassy to do so in any manner either covertly or overtly.

There is a need to engage this very pro-Indian group of opinion shapers and their families to ensure a continuous favourable opinion. We must develop some formal engagement systems to continue to engage with these very vocal, influential opinion shapers who function in the small spread-out rural communities of Nepal and continue to explain to them the reasons of various Indian actions. Today, it is essential that public opinion towards India must continually be re-shaped and a favourable opinion be driven, especially in this connected world. We no longer have the luxury of not doing so.

It is in India's interests to help Nepal find solutions to their problems. When faced with a common enemy, the monarchy, which threatened them with extinction in 2005-2006, all the parties in Nepal came together, and in the bargain, a long-running insurgency also ended. All bilateral efforts must lead to a closer people-to-people relationship. This is the most vital aspect of bilateral relations and can only be ignored at India's peril. As a long-term strategy, India needs to understand the wishes of the people of Nepal and tailor its policy accordingly.

The Government of Nepal and the ruling coalition must use all mechanisms to restore trust with the Madhesi and Tharu populations by forming an independent mechanism to investigate the protest-related deaths and avoid a heavy-handed security response during protests. Further, they must with great sensitivity, refrain from announcing ultimatums and provocative comments and address the very real economic and humanitarian consequences of earthquakes and blockades. Further, all Nepali political parties must agree urgently on terms of reference for a mechanism on state boundaries and postpone local elections if there is no roadmap to address constitutional disagreements.

The current situation is a creation of the past and a precursor to the future. Since, the histories, as well as the present socio-political and economic scenario of not only India and Nepal, but also all the South Asian nations are interlinked and inseparable, based on their close geographical proximity, related historical developments, and interdependency, hence, it is crucial that the nations continue to work towards mutual cooperation and understanding so that such reciprocity of shared interests would continue to grow and strengthen future bonds. This approach would successfully assume a great power and unifying role in South Asia and beyond.

NOTES

1. Ibid.
2. Tharakan, P.K.H. This Time in Kathmandu, *Indian Express*, 5 July 2010, p. 2.
3. Ibid.
4. Dixit, K.M. Letting Nepal Be, *The Hindu*, 15 September 2016 at http://www.thehindu.com/opinion/lead/Letting-Nepal-be/article14374584.ece accessed on 2 March 2017.
5. Dixit, K.M. (15 September 2016). Letting Nepal Be,. *The Hindu*, retrieved from http://www.thehindu.com/opinion/lead/Letting-Nepal-be/article14374584.ece
6. Ibid.
7. Authors presence in Indian Embassy, Nepal (2004-2007).

BIBLIOGRAPHY

Primary Sources

Interviews with the ambassadors of India and Nepal, retired Army Chiefs, and Indian Army Ex-Servicemen of Nepali origin in Nepal.

Reports

Chhetri, D. (1996a), Educationally Disadvantaged Ethnic Groups of Nepal. MIMAP-I Project, Agricultural Projects Services Centre Kathmandu, Nepal. Unpublished Report.

CIA – The World Factbook. *Field Listing-Disputes-International.* Produced by CIAs Directorate of Intelligence, United States of America.

Crisis Group Asia Report No149. *Nepal's Election and Beyond.* 2 April 2008.

DESA, UN. (2016). United Nations Department of Economic and Social Affairs/Statistics Division. Population and Vital Statistics Report. *Statistical Papers Series* A, vol., LXVIII.

Embassy of Nepal. *Socio Cultural Relations*, New Delhi.

Hodgson to Govt. of India. 26 May 1838. Foreign Dept Sec, 13 June 1838, No. 10, NAI.

ICIMOD (International Centre for Integrated Mountain Development). 1997. *New Era,* Nepal.

International Boundary Study (No. 50-30 May 1965). *China – Nepal Boundary.* Office of the Geographer, Bureau of Intelligence and Research, United States of America.

Ministry of External Affairs, Government of India. (2013). *A Note on India-Nepal.* Ministry of External Affairs: New Delhi.

Ministry of External Affairs, Government of India. (2013). *Fact sheet –*

India and Nepal Partnership. Ministry of External Affairs, New Delhi.

Nepal Electricity Authority (NEA). (2014). *Nationwide Master Plan Study on Storage-type Hydroelectric Power Development in Nepal: Final Report Summary.* Japan International Cooperation Agency, Electric Power Development Co., Ltd.

Report of the Legislative Parliament Committee for International Relations and Human Rights, Constituent Assembly. 2008, Nepal.

UNMIN (United Nations Mission in Nepal). 2 October 2012. *The United Nations and Nepal's Peace Process*. UNMIN.

Books

Bhasin, A.S. (ed.). (1997). *Nepal's relations with India and China: documents 1947-1992*. Siba Exim, New Delhi.

Bose, S. & Jalal, A. (2004). *Modern South Asia: history, culture, political economy*. Psychology Press, New Delhi.

Daniels, P.T. & Bright, W. (eds.). (1996). *The Worlds Writing Systems*. Oxford University Press, New Delhi.

Dharamdasani, M.D. (1976). *Indian diplomacy in Nepal*. Aalekh Publishers, Jaipur.

Dubey, M. (2013). *India's Foreign Policy: Coping with the Changing World.* Pearson, Delhi.

Gould, T. (1999). *Imperial warriors: Britain and the Gurkhas*. Granta Books, London.

Gyawali, D. (1995). Himalayan Waters: Between Euphoric Dreams and Ground Realities. In K. Bahadur & M. Lama (eds.), *New Perspective on India-Nepal Relations*. Har-Anand Publications, New Delhi.

Hall, D.M. & Elliman, D. (eds.). (2006). *Health for all children.* Revised fourth edition. Oxford University Press.

Helble, M. (2007). On The Influence of World Religions on International Trade. Graduates Institute of International Studies. University of Geneva, Switzerland.

Jha, B.K. (1973). *Indo-Nepalese Relations, 1951-1972*. Vora, Bombay.

Katti, V. (2001). *Indo-Nepal Trade: Post WTO Dimension*. Kalinga Publishers, New Delhi.

Mehta, A.K. (2001). Problems of Terrorism and Other Illegal Activities on the Indo-Nepal Border: Issues in Effective Border Management. In

Ramakant and B.C. Upreti (eds.) *India and Nepal: Aspects of Interdependent Relations*. Kalinga Publications, Delhi.

Muni, S.D. (1973). *Foreign Policy of Nepal*. National Publishing House, Delhi.

Muni, S.D. (1977). The Dynamics of Foreign Policy. In D. Muni (ed.), *Nepal: Assertive Monarchy*. Chetana Publications, Delhi.

Muni, S.D. & Chadha, V. (2014). *Asian Strategic Review 2015: India as a Security Provider*. Pentagon Press, New Delhi.

Nayak, N.R. (2014). *Strategic Himalayas: Republican Nepal and External Powers*. Pentagon Press, New Delhi.

Negi, S.S. (1991). *Himalayan Rivers, Lakes and Glaciers*. Indus Publishing Co., New Delhi.

Rai, B. (2009). *Gorkhas: The Warrior Race*. Kalpaz Publications, Delhi.

Rajbahak, R.P. (1992). *Nepal-India Open Border*. Lancer Publishers Pvt. Ltd., New Delhi.

Ramesh, J. (2005). *Making sense of Chindia: reflections on China and India*. India Research Press.

Rana, P.S.J.B. (1971). *Nepal's Fourth Plan: a Critique*. Yeti Pocket Books, Kathmandu.

Rangachari, R. (1995). Water Resources Management in India-Nepal Cooperation. In K. Bahadur & M. Lama (eds.), *New Perspective on India-Nepal Relations*. Har-Anand Publications, New Delhi.

Ray, H. (1983). *China's strategy in Nepal*. Radiant Publishers, New Delhi.

Rose, L.E. (1971). *Nepal Strategy for Survival*. Oxford University Press, Bombay.

Savada, A.M. (ed.). (1991). *Nepal: A Country Study*. Washington, GPO for the Library of Congress.

Scott, D. (ed.). (2011). *Handbook of India's international relations*. Routledge, Delhi.

Shah, S.K. (2017). *India's Foreign Policy: Past, Present and Ties with the World*. Vij Books India Pvt. Ltd., Delhi.

Singh, A.K. (2004). *Restructuring of Nepali State: A Madheshi Perspective*. Nepal Centre for Contemporary Studies.

Stiller, L.F. (1973). *The rise of the house of Gorkha: a study in the unification of Nepal, 1768-1816*. Mañjusri Pub. House, New Delhi.

Thapliyal, S. (1998). *Mutual Security: The case of India-Nepal*. Lancer Publishers, New Delhi.

Van Kemenade, W. (2008). *Détente between China and India: The Delicate Balance of Geopolitics in Asia.* Netherlands Institute of International Relations, Clingendael.

Van Schaik, S. (2011). *Tibet: A history.* Yale University Press, London.

Yogi, N.N. & Acharya, B. (eds.). (1951). *Rashtrapita Shri 5 Bada Maharaj Prithvi Narayan Shah Divyopadesh.* Divine Council of Shri 5 Maharaj Prithvi Narayan Shah the Great, Kathmandu.

Journal Articles

Baral, L.R. (1986). Nepal's Security Policy and South Asian Regionalism. *Asian Survey*, 26(11).

Chamberlain, A., Cambon, J., von Kühlmann, R., & Davis, J. W. (1931). The Permanent Bases of German Foreign Policy. *Foreign Affairs* (An American Quarterly Review), 9(2):179-194.

Ghoble. (1985). China-Nepal Relations and India. *Asian Survey,* 25(5).

Gyawali, D. & Dixit, D. (1999). Mahakali Impasse and Indo-Nepal Water Conflict. *Economic & Political Weekly*, 553-564.

Jayasundara, N.S. (2014). The development of language education policy: An Indian Perspective; a view from Tamil Nadu. *International Journal of Scientific and Research Publications,* 4(11).

Kumar, S. (2011). China's Expanding Footprint in Nepal: Threats to India. *Journal of Defence Studies,* 5(2): 77-89.

Manchanda, R. (2001). Neighbours: Business not as usual: India-Nepal trade relations force another round of turbulence. *Frontline*, 18(8): 63-64.

Raman, B. (2009). Seeing China from Chengdu. *South Asia Analysis Group (SAAG)*, 2381.

Singh, R.S.N. (2010). The China Factor in Nepal. *Indian Defence Review*, 25: 2.

Sujit, D. (2008). Sino-Indian Relations and Some Issues. *Strategic Analysis*, 11(11).

Tiwary, R. (2006). Indo-Nepal Water Resource Negotiation: Deepening Divide over Border Project (Globalization and Particularism in South Asia). *South Asian Journal*, 11.

Verma, B. (2010). Nightmare 2012: Chinese Special Forces cut off Siliguri corridor. *Indian Defence Review*, 25(2).

Verma, B. (2011). Threat from China. *Indian Defence Review,* 23.2.

Internet Sources/e-news

Adhikary, D. (17 November 2009. Political impasse takes Nepal to brink. *Asia Times*. Retrieved from http://yubabahas.com/?p=20795

Aneja, A. (20 August 2016). Myanmar to support Silk Road, BCIM. *The Hindu*. Retrieved from http://www.thehindu.com/news/international/Myanmar-to-support-Silk-Road-BCIM/article14580511.ece

Bajpai, K. (11 December 2010). The Chinese Are Coming. *The Times of India*. Retrieved from http://timesofindia.indiatimes.com/edit-page/The-Chinese-Are-Coming/articleshow/7078878.cms

Bhamuik, S. (May 2005). Guns, Drugs and Rebels. *Seminar*, 550. Retrieved from http://www.india-seminar.com/2005/550/550%20subir%20 bhaumik.htm

Bhattacharya, A. (23 May 2008). China and Maoist Nepal: Challenges for India. *Institute for Defence Studies and Analyses*. Retrieved from http://www.idsa.in/idsastrategiccomments/ChinaandMaoistNepal_ABhattacharya_230508

Bhattacharya, A. (18 May 2009). China's Inroads into Nepal: India's Concerns. *Institute for Defence Studies and Analyses*. Retrieved from http://www.idsa.in/idsastrategiccomments/ChinasInroadsintoNepal_ABhattacharya_180509

Chinese leaders caution Baidya against foreign interests in federalism (26 July 2012). *Nepal News*. Retrieved from http://www.nepalnews.com/archive/2012/jul/jul26/news18.php

Dahal returns from China; prescribes trilateral talks for strategy on Nepal (27 October 2010). *Nepal News*. Retrieved from http://www.nepalnews.com/home/index.php/news/2/10090-dahalreturns-from China

Defining Himalayan borders an uphill battle (3 January 2000). *Asian Political News*. Retrieved from http://findarticles.com/p/articles/mi_m0WDQ/is_2000-Jan-3/ai_58533253/

Dixit, K. M. (15 September 2016). Letting Nepal Be. *The Hindu*. Retrieved from http://www.thehindu.com/opinion/lead/Letting-Nepal-be/article14374584.ece

Duquesne, I. (25 October 2012). Nepal: The China Card. *Telegraph Nepal*. Retrieved from http://www.telegraphnepal.com/national/2012-10-25/nepal:-the-china-card-

Farzand, A. (19 June 2000). Nepal: Wake-Up Call, Interview: CP Bastol. *India Today*. Retrieved from http://www.india.today.com/itoday/20000619/neighbours.html

Gajurel, C.P. (25 December 2008). No Special relation between Nepal and India. *The Telegraph Weekly*. Retrieved from http://www.telegraph nepal.com/backup/telegraph/news_det.php?news_ id+4576

Gurung, H. (26 August 2010). Nepali Nationalism. *Telegraph Nepal*. Retrieved from http://www.telegraphnepal.com/news_det.php?news_id=2080

India's Boundary Disputes with China, Nepal, and Pakistan (15 May 1998). *International Boundary Monitor*. Retrieved from http://www.boundaries.com/India.htm

India ready to renegotiate 1950 treaty with Nepal (6 May 2008). *One India News*. Retrieved from http://news.oneindia.in/2008/05/06/india-ready-to-renegotiate-1950-treaty-with-nepal 1210072316.html

India sees red over UN officials meet with Nepal Maoists (7 November 2007). *The Times of India*. Retrieved from http://timesofindia.india times.com/india/India-sees-red-over-UN-officials-meet-with-Nepal-Maoists/articleshow/2529830.cms?

Jha, H.B. (24 September 2015). Nepal's New Constitution: An Analysis from the Madheshi Perspective. *Institute for Defence Studies and Analyses*. Retrieved from http://www.idsa.in/idsacomments/NepalsNewConsti tution_hbjha_240915

Jha, P. (2 October 2012). One country two armies situation ends in Nepal. *The Hindu*. Retrieved from http://www.thehindu.com/news/international/%E2%80%98One-country-two-armies%E2%80%99-situation-ends-in-Nepal/article12542632.ece

Karna, V.K. (20 March 2007). Madhesh and Madheshi: A Geographical and Historic Perspective. *Madhesi*. Retrieved from https://madhesi.wordpress.com/2007/03/20/madhesh-and-madheshi-a-geographical-and-historic-perspective/

Lee, P. (14 November 2009). Sino-Indian rivalry fuels Nepal's turmoil. *Asia Times*. Retrieved from http://www.atimes.com/atimes/South_Asia/KK14Df01.html

Nayak, N. (30 March 2009). Nepal: New Strategic Partner of China? *Institute for Defence Studies and Analyses*. Retrieved from http://www.idsa.in/

idsastrategiccomments/NepalNewStrategicPartnerofChina_NNayak_300309

Nepal wont jeopardise any genuine Indian interest (3 September 2011). *The Hindu*. Retrieved from http://www.thehindu.com/opinion/interview/article2419048.ece

PM in Norway, holds talks on energy deal (29 March 2009). *The Rising Nepal.* Retrieved from http://democracyandclasstruggle.blogspot.in/2009/03/prime-minister-prachanda-innorway.html

Rana, M. S. J. B. (29 July 2011). Sino-Nepal Relations: Economic Agenda for a 21st Century Strategic Partnership. *The Himalayan Voice.* Retrieved from https://thehimalayanvoice.wordpress.com/2011/07/29/sino-nepal-relations-economic-agenda-for-a-21st-century-strategic-partnership/

Saran, S. (17 March 2010). Premature power. *Business Standard.* Retrieved from http://www.business-standard.com/article/opinion/shyam-saran-premature-power-110031700019_1.html

Shah, S.G. (21 February 2006). Social Inclusion of Madheshi Community in Nation Building. *Democracy for Nepal.* Retrieved from http://demrepubnepal.blogspot.in/2006/02/govind-shah-social-inclusion-of.html

Sharma, G. (10 March 2017). Anti-India Protests erupt in Nepal over shooting death on border. *Reuters.* Retrieved from http://www.reuters.com/article/us-nepal-india/anti-india-protests-erupt-in-nepal-over-shooting-death-on-border-idUSKBN16H1CS

Shrestha, P.J. (1 February 2010). What is Sugauli Treaty? *AIMSA Collection for Study.* Retrieved from http://ramkshrestha.wordpress.com/2010/02/01/sugauli-treaty/

Sundaraman, S. (15 December 2010). The dragons teeth. *The Asian Age.* Retrieved from http://archive.asianage.com/columnists/dragon%E2%80%99s-teeth-535

Thakur, S. (3 May 2008). Nepal to Delhi: Junk sentiment and special ties. *The Telegraph.* Retrieved from https://www.telegraphindia.com/1080503/jsp/nation/story_9219398.jsp

Tharakan, P.K.H. (5 July 2010). This time in Kathmandu. *The Indian Express.* Retrieved from http://indianexpress.com/article/opinion/columns/this-time-in-kathmandu/

Vision for tomorrow: India–Nepal Ties (29 April 2013). *República.* Retrieved from http://www.myrepublica.com/portal/index.php?action=news_details&news_id=53965

While India sleeps, Chinese threat grows (May 26 2008). *Rediff.com News.* Retrieved from http://www.rediff.com/news/column/guest/20080526.htm

Why India needs to fine-tune its ties with Nepal (22 November 2011). *Rediff.com News.* Retrieved from http://www.rediff.com/news/column/why-india-needs-to-fine-tune-its-ties-with-nepal/20111122.htm

Wolfe, A. (3 February 2006). Nepal's Instability in the Regional Power Struggle. *Power and Interest News Report.* Retrieved from http://www.worldproutassembly.org/archives/2006/02/nepals_instabil.html

Internet Sources/ e-magazines/ e-blogs

Arpi, Claude. (30 January 2015). The shadowy Mr. Xiao. *Claude Arpi Blog.* Retrieved from http://claudearpi.blogspot.in/2015/01/

Basnet, P. (April 2011). China's Success. *Himal South Asian.* Retrieved from http://himalmag.com/component/content/article/4350-chinas-success-html

Bezem. (January 2015). Perspective of Nepal and Nepal Army History Essay. *Bezern.* Retrieved from https://www.bezem.com/read-power-115578.htm

Bhattari, R. (January 2005). Geopolitical specialties of Nepal and international approach to conflict transformation. *Nepal Foreign Affairs.* Retrieved from http://nepalforeignaffairs.com/geopolitical-specialties-of-nepal-and-international-approach-to-conflict-transformation/

Bohara, R. (September 2015). War-makers to peace-keepers. *Nepali Times,* 774. Retrieved from http://nepalitimes.com/article/nation/Nepal-from-war-makers-to-peace-keepers,2565

Gandhi, I. (October 1972). India and the World. *Foreign Affairs.* Retrieved from https://www.foreignaffairs.com/articles/asia/1972-10-01/india-and-world

Karki, R. (3 February 2016). Lessons Unlearnt. *República.* Retrieved from http://e.myrepublica.com/2015/index.php?option=com_k2&view=item&id=36372:lessons-unlearnt&Itemid=267

Lal, C. K. (August-September 2007). Political ecology of the madhes. *Nepali Times,* 364. Retrieved from www.nepalitimes.com/issue/364/StateoftheState/13907

Murthy, P. (September 2009). Time to Reassess Indo-Nepal Relations. *Institute of Peace and Conflict Studies,* 2965. Retrieved from http://www.ipcs.org/article/south-asia/time-to-reassess-indo-nepal-relations-2965.html

Ranade, J. (February 2014). China's Tightening Embrace of Nepal. Retrieved from https://www.facebook.com/unfftNEPAL/posts/708983772467140

Verma, J.K. (August 2013). India to Resume arms supply to Nepal – Bilateral Relations to improve on all fronts. *India Strategic.* Retrieved from http://www.indiastrategic.in/topstories2098_India_resume_ arms_supply_Nepal.htm.

Other Internet Sources

Birendra P. Mishra, http://www.thehimalayantimes.com/ dated 5 August 2014.

Democracy for Nepal. http://derepubnepal.blogspot.com/

Economic Dependency on China, sources: http://www.hrw.org/English/docs/2005/' 1/28/Nepal.htm, http://www.cia.gov.np/bilateral/Nepal-china

http://knowledge.whatron.upenn.edu/public policy As Tension Sweeps the Terai Plains, Nepal Tilts Toward China.

Norman, 1965, p. 269.

Pioneer. New Delhi, 20 August 2001.

Prashant Jha. *Hindustan Times,* 13 August 2014, http://www.Hindustan times.com/

Tibetan Review. August 2008, pp. 23-24.

Websites

http://www.nepalarmy.mil.np/

http://www.mofa.gov.np/en/nepalsforeign-policy-102.html

http://www.fmprc.gov.cn/eng/wjdt/2649/t649608.htm

http://www.indianembassy.org.np

http://www.umass.edu/rso/fretibet/education.html

http://www.indiandefencereview.com/2010/05

https://www.globalsecurity.org/military/world/nepal/climate.htm

INDEX